CORNERSTONES | VOL. 2
GOSPEL WITNESS

CORNERSTONES

VOL. 1
GOSPEL CULTURE: LIVING IN GOD'S KINGDOM
JOSEPH BOOT

VOL. 2
GOSPEL WITNESS: DEFENDING & EXTENDING THE KINGDOM OF GOD
JOSEPH BOOT

CORNERSTONES | VOL. 2

GOSPEL WITNESS

DEFENDING & EXTENDING THE KINGDOM OF GOD

JOSEPH BOOT

Wilberforce Publications
London

First published in Canada in 2017 by
Ezra Press

Second edition published in Great Britain in 2017 by
Wilberforce Publications Limited
70 Wimpole Street, London W1G 8AX
in association with the
Ezra Institute for Contemporary Christianity, Canada

Book design by Steve Oakley

Printed in the UK by Imprint Digital, Exeter
and worldwide by Createspace

ISBN 978-0-9956832-6-6

TO J. JOHN
Early mentor, life-long friend, and outstanding example of gospel witness

CONTENTS

Foreword
to *Gospel Witness*

In these short but packed chapters Dr. Joe Boot most helpfully presents the modern reader with a profound analysis of the three systems that oppose belief in the truth of the Bible in our time—*secularism, religious paganism* and *Islam*. None of the three are modern, but they present themselves in our time with great force in the religious confusion of the present world, which sooner or later Christians must face. The book is appropriately called *Gospel Witness* because what the world needs now is apologetic witness.

Joe identifies the rationalist or secular humanist as one of the significant opponents to Christian belief today. Oddly enough, as Joe argues, this person who rejects belief and only wants rational arguments, depends on *faith* to make those rational arguments. The fact is, you have to believe that reason is rational before you make rational arguments. But like the syncretist, for whom there is no place above the mountain, there is no place outside of rational discourse where the rationalist can objectively stand.

If this intrigues you, you must read on.

Next, a further devastating critique of religious tolerance undermines the appeals of modern day religious paganism that claims to bring peace to the world. Joe asks where would one need to be located to know, as religious pagans claim, "that all paths on a mountain lead to the top? The only location that would allow such a perspective is high above the mountain. So the seemingly humble assertion of modern religious syncretism amounts to an objective claim to an absolute divine perspective," derived from the god within. Clearly the religious syncretist pretends to occupy a position of neutrality. In fact, such a person claims to possess absolute knowledge, a claim which is clearly false. This is the way that "pluralistic man," implicitly or explicitly claiming to be divine, illegitimately promotes religious syncretism that so we all 'just get along.' Joe shows that this religion hails from the rebel Nimrod and the Tower of Babel, that is, from rank rejection of God the Creator that leads to spiritual, ethical and sexual confusion and ultimate destruction. This is where present day all-is-one spirituality will end up.

Third, Joe provides a devastating but fair analysis of Islam as a Oneist and totalitarian system that ultimately must apply its system by force upon those who resist. He convincingly shows that Islam is not a religion that can be blended with Christianity, but a religion that in its early days took an originally pagan doctrine of god as an unknown and supreme *principle of fate* (like *karma* in the nature religions) and superimposed this idea upon the Old Testament notion of a transcendent, personal God who speaks into history. But Islam's rejection of the Trinity as polytheistic means that Allah emerges as a radically impersonal Monad or Singularity. Such a god must depend upon the creation and in this case upon the humanly fallible Muhammad for any notion of personhood. Of course, a creator dependent on the creation must give up any claim to divine transcendence and thus to true divinity.

Joe Boot has his finger on the pulse of modern apologetics, which he has developed in many places. Essentially his argument in this important short book, which is the fruit of that thinking, is that whether you are a Muslim following a system contrived by an obviously human Muhammad, a spiritual mystic following your own god within, or a rationalist creating your own "intelligent" answer, there is really no place to stand in a world created by God the Triune Creator except a place of faith in the God Who makes sense of everything. We humans occupy a universe so vast that we did not make and cannot understand apart from a clear word from the One who made it, and who, in the person of the Son, has redeemed it. Joe ends this call to witness with a powerful appeal to remember that Christian witness also involves deeds of mercy, and leaves us with the example of William Wilberforce who brought an end to the slave trade in Britain, and who was convinced that "Christianity must be allowed to pervade and penetrate every corner of a Christian's existence."

Joe has done the church a great service in this brief work of cultural apologetics.

PETER JONES
Professor Emeritus of Greek and New Testament,
Westminster Theological Seminary, Escondido,
 and Director of truthXchange

PREFACE
TO THE SERIES

The Ezra Institute for Contemporary Christianity (EICC) is an evangelical Christian organization dedicated to two great objects. First, the preservation and advancement of the truth, freedom and beauty of the gospel, and second, the renewal of culture in terms of the lordship of Jesus Christ.

The gospel of the kingdom, resting as it does upon Christ's declaration of jubilee, is alone the source of true freedom, righteousness and justice. As well, the gospel is all-encompassing in scope, a leaven that permeates and informs every area of life and thought. Regarding this comprehensive truth of full salvation, Jesus himself declared, "If the Son sets you free, you shall be free indeed" (John 8:36).

Throughout history the Lord has entrusted the work of gospel-centred culture building and renewal to his people (Genesis 1:28; 9:1; Matthew 28:18–20). This task is particularly urgent in our day because the organs and institutions of modern culture have been thoroughly saturated by humanistic and pagan assumptions about the source and nature of truth and freedom. These pretensions have steadily redefined intellectual, social, familial, sexual and ethical norms, unleashing real evil and enslaving Western society in a radical opposition to Christ and the freedom brought by the gospel. From the school, academy and courthouse, to senates, parliaments and palaces, the Christian faith is being systematically expunged from public life and ignored or assaulted in our corridors of learning and power. If we love the gospel, our neighbours and freedom, Christians must take up the cultural task with faith and courage.

The EICC is committed to bringing a comprehensive gospel to bear on all of life, challenging and serving culture-shapers in all spheres, resourcing and equipping Christian leaders and professionals in public life and teaching believers to understand and advance the truth, beauty and freedom of the gospel in all its varied implications. By encouraging and intellectually resourcing Christian engagement with culture, we believe that biblical truth can once again captivate hearts and minds, and shape our future to the glory of God (Philippians 1:7; Colossians 1:15–20).

The *Cornerstones* series of short, focused monographs, published by Ezra Press, is intended to be an accessible point of entry for thoughtful Christians wishing to develop and/or strengthen their understanding of the scope and implications of the gospel, and of the particular but timeless challenges to that gospel being posed by non-Christian thought in the twenty-first century. From there, our hope is that this initiative will be further used of the Lord to animate, encourage and strengthen the public witness and testimony of God's church, so that she might live up to her calling as the pillar and support of the truth (1 Timothy 3:15), so that through the church, the manifold wisdom of God might be made known (Ephesians 3:10).

RANDALL CURRIE
Board Chair, Ezra Institute for Contemporary Christianity

1

THE CONTEXT: THE CULTURAL CHALLENGE IN THE WEST

"YOU WILL BE MY WITNESSES IN JERUSALEM, IN ALL JUDEA AND SAMARIA, AND TO THE ENDS OF THE EARTH" (ACTS 1:8).

FACING THE NEW ORTHODOXY

It has been rightly said that the loves of a few men move the lives of many. The deeply-held convictions of a zealous minority, tenaciously pursued, are culturally formative—at times for good, and at times for ill. Culture has been variously defined, but Henry Van Til's succinct description of culture as "religion externalized" is, in my judgment, the most helpful and accurate: culture is the manifestation of a society's faith or ultimate commitment, expressed in everything from art and architecture to politics and literature.[1] In our own time,

---

[1] Henry Van Til, *The Calvinistic Concept of Culture* (Grand Rapids: Baker, 1972), 200. For a thorough introduction to the relationship of Christianity to culture see the

there can be no denying the staggering success of an anti-Christian political religion that has, especially over the past sixty years, steadily overturned what were, previously, broadly Christian institutions, laws and cultural mores.

Indeed, this anti-Christian cultural movement has made a special point of challenging every scripturally-rooted creational norm— right down to the foundations of life's sanctity, the nature of marriage, sexuality, and human identity as constituted by the binaries of male and female. Things *literally unthinkable* to my grandparents' generation have become established social orthodoxy, and heretics are increasingly being punished by censure, exclusion, shaming, ostracism, legal threats, human rights commissions, loss of social standing, loss of employment and even loss of liberty behind bars if reparations are not made. The seemingly unstoppable and rapid advance of this neo-Marxist and neo-pagan worldview, aided by a largely unprepared and ineffective church pulpit, means a religious revolution has left many Christians stunned, confused and often afraid to do anything but retreat or concede. In such a context, faithful gospel witness looks distinctly like courage, while compromise looks more and more like cowardice.

In his 2016 book *The Demon in Democracy: Totalitarian Temptations in Free Societies*, the Polish philosopher and politician Ryszard Legutko offers a penetrating analysis of the religion of liberal democracy and the gradual decay of western states into increasingly oppressive, revolutionary societies, in the influential grip of a committed cultural elite. These 'progressive' societies, he argues, are increasingly manifesting a remarkable and indeed disturbing similarity in character to the former communist regime in Eastern Europe.

On this new homogenization of acceptable opinion, he notes that

unfortunately, since the transformation of democracy into a liberal democracy, the spectrum of political acceptability has been distinctly limited. Liberal democracy has created its own

---

first Cornerstones volume: Joseph Boot, *Gospel Culture: Living in God's Kingdom* (Toronto: Ezra Press, 2016).

orthodoxy... [and] a political mechanism for the election of people, organizations and ideas in line with the orthodoxy.[2]

The allusion to a difference between democracy and *liberal* democracy refers to the fact that there is nothing peculiarly or ideologically 'liberal' about political organization involving the consent of the people to be governed, their participation in that government, and the democratic attempt to limit the concentration of power in any one individual or institution. There were early experiments with democracy in ancient Greece that were not 'liberal' by any modern standard and both the Whigs and Tories in English political life supported Parliamentary democracy. But modern *liberal* democracy invokes a particular ideological vision to be attached to government by consent. It is "a powerful unifying mechanism, blurring differences between people and imposing uniformity of views, behaviour and language.... The impetus of liberalism was understood to lie in its cooperative feature, which was to bring the human race to a higher stage of development."[3] This concept of bringing man to higher stages of development by political means is of a religious character. So, while recognizing there remain substantial pockets of resistance to this contemporary faith, modern liberal democracy, with its egalitarian worldview, has become a *de facto* cultural religion with the power to discipline nonconformists.

Recognizing a variety of historical forces giving shape to this homogenous 'new orthodoxy,' Legutko identifies the political revolutions of the 1960s as having had the decisive impact, moving an impatient utopian and collectivist radicalism into a position of cultural dominance. He comments,

> The language of the revolution was a medley of anarchist slogans, a Marxist rhetoric of class struggle and the overthrowing of capitalism, and a liberal language of rights, emancipation, and discrimination. Capitalism and the state were the main

---

[2] Ryszard Legutko, *The Demon in Democracy: Totalitarian Temptations in Free Societies* (New York: Encounter Books, 2016), 82.

[3] Legutko, *The Demon in Democracy*, 3, 17.

targets, but universities, schools, family, law and social mores were attacked with equal vehemence.[4]

He points out that this ideological movement has continued into the present, and grown to the point where the worldview has become institutionalized and entrenched.

NEW QUESTIONS AND A NEW SITUATION

This gradual sea-change in our culture's underlying religious assumptions has logically led to significant variation in the *types of questions* or objections people now have regarding the Christian faith, thereby impacting the task of Christian witness as we think about faithful evangelism and apologetics. A generation ago, people's questions and objections tended to focus on things like the historicity of the resurrection, the authenticity of the New Testament text, or the plausibility of miraculous claims in Scripture. Now, younger people especially are typically unconcerned with denying miracles, but will often object that Christianity is too exclusive, oppressive and intolerant, or that it has an imperialist history with blood on its hands. Christianity is deemed irrelevant, outmoded and untrue, not because there is a lack of evidence for the resurrection, but because Christians don't appear to advance 'equality' or 'saving the planet,' reducing carbon footprints by any means—including abortion. This generation, indoctrinated from elementary school in the thought forms of radical progressives from Herbert Marcuse to Judith Butler (all rooted in neo-Marxist philosophical assumptions), wants to know why anyone would believe in a God that discriminates against women, denies her the right to choose, and excludes practicing homosexuals and other members of the queer community from the kingdom of God—a God who doesn't advance 'social justice' in the world just isn't worth believing in. Some Christians have felt so overwhelmed or intimidated by the apparent force of these objections, that they have either stopped witnessing to the truth of the gospel or have been 'converted' themselves, seeking to synthesize Christianity with the cultural religion of the age.

---

[4] Legutko, *The Demon in Democracy*, 83.

COMPLACENCY AND COMPROMISE

How is it that Christians have been caught so off-guard and flat-footed in our revolutionary times? Why has our witness been so muted and often ineffective? There are many things that could be said about this question, but one important answer is that, in general, Christian believers in the West have *lacked vigilance* and so neglected the development and defense of a consistently scriptural vision of reality in the wake of our remarkable historic success in evangelizing and shaping Western cultural life.

In other words, we too readily assumed that broadly Christian norms would hold; that largely Christian categories of life and thought, established by centuries of tradition, would remain the religious presuppositions of the people; that a robustly developed scriptural philosophy and cultural apologetic were unnecessary because Christian assumptions were now simply 'common sense' assumptions; that the task of evangelization on our own shores was largely done and the sacrifices of the past no longer necessary. Biblical laws were really 'natural laws'—surely agreed upon by all 'civilized' people—and the Christian view of life and truth, liberty and justice was in fact an essentially neutral perspective received by every 'rational' state in terms of God's common grace. In short, we thought we need no longer contend for being distinctly Christian or explicitly directed by biblical revelation as a culture, because people already accepted broadly Christian ideas. In the insightful words of Peter Hitchens,

> It was the triumph of the Christian religion that for many centuries it managed to become the unreasoning assumption of almost all, built into every spoken and written word, every song, and every building. It was the disaster of the Christian religion that it assumed this triumph would last forever and outlast everything, and so it was ill equipped to resist the challenge of a rival when it came, in this, the century of the self. The Christian religion had no idea that a new power, which I call selfism, would arise. And, having arisen, selfism has easily shouldered its rival aside. In free competition, how can a faith based upon self-restraint and patience compete with one that pardons, uncon-

ditionally and in advance, all the self-indulgences you can think of, and some you cannot?[5]

In the face of what Hitchens here memorably calls *selfism*, where every man is his own god (Genesis 3:5), we have quickly capitulated, our witness dying out with a whimper. With all moral restraint cast to the wind, who can resist? First, we *gradually withdrew* from faithful witness in the fields of conflict in family, education, law, politics, art and every other sphere. Soon thereafter we began justifying our abandonment of a distinctly Christian vision for life in the world altogether, settling for the 'neutral' status quo and retreating into the four walls of the church. But even there many began claiming that surrender, synthesis or compromise with the new religious power was the better part of valour for the 'survival' of the faith—a faith that by this point had become radically altered and increasingly unrecognizable. At this steep trajectory of declension we should not be surprised, for once you have self-consciously abdicated the Lordship of Jesus Christ in one sphere of life, you will eventually surrender your witness to it everywhere.

In a damning display of irony, it so happened that with the collapse of our biblical witness—the various spheres of culture effectively abandoned—and the Christian's life in the world dominated by a secular, even pagan vision, the church itself soon became radically politicized, so that challenging the Christian in the pew about the issues of life that matter most has come to be considered offensive and unacceptable. To witness faithfully regarding beginning and end of life issues, biblical marriage, sexuality, family, education, law, political and cultural life etc. in terms of the light of God's Word is seen by many as a violation of church-state separation, an invasion of privacy, or a political offense as though the church were a 'safe space' to escape the convicting voice of God himself.

And so pastors and their pulpits *bend* to what their people want to hear. But, "has not the greatest danger always been that those charged with the duty of preaching the steep and rugged pathway persuade themselves that weakness is compassion, and that sin can be cured

---

5   Peter Hitchens, "The Fantasy of Addiction," *First Things*, last modified February 2017, https://www.firstthings.com/article/2017/02/the-fantasy-of-addiction.

at a clinic, or soothed with a pill? And so falsehood flourishes in great power, like the green bay tree."[6] These present circumstances remind me of some words quoted by Aragorn in J. R. R. Tolkien's *Lord of the Rings*, in which he laments the collapse of the realm of Rohan:

> Where now the horse and the rider?
>   Where is the horn that was blowing?
> …They have passed like rain on the mountain,
>   like a wind in the meadow;
> The days have gone down in the West
>   behind the hills into shadow.[7]

NEW COURAGE OF OLD CONVICTIONS

In the face of the great retreat and surrender of the Western Christian church in our time it is difficult to confront the cutting words of Hendrik Marsman, who suggested that the Christian believer:

> will in practice always be an enemy of the art of poetry, and Christianity of culture. When things become tense or oppressive, the Christian withdraws, with or without pretence, back to the kingdom that is not of this world and leaves us, including the poets, alone, with the chestnuts still in the fire. This is also what makes the Christian an unreliable player in the affairs of this world, particularly in culture, and especially from the Protestant one can expect nothing when push comes to shove. He is constantly ready to flee.[8]

This is a terrible indictment and one which has too often come *awfully close* to the truth, when cowardice is dressed as piety and faithless flight as innovation and progress.

Yet at its root the challenge of our time is not really new, and the historic record of many Christians who walked as men of Issachar in

---

[6] Hitchens, "The Fantasy of Addiction."

[7] J.R.R. Tolkien, *The Two Towers: Being the second part of The Lord of the Rings* (London: Harper Collins, 2014), 141–42.

[8] Henrik Marsman, cited in C. Van Der Waal, *The World our Home: Christians between Creation and Recreation*, trans. Gerda Jacobi, ed. Conrad Van Dyk (Neerlandia, Alberta: Inheritance Publications, 2013), 52.

the face of persecution and oppression is better than Marsman is perhaps aware of or ready to admit.[9] The idea that we are the first Christians called to witness in a radically hostile culture, to be considered 'haters of humanity,' or to find that sexual culture, human identity, life, truth and justice are being defined in a profoundly unbiblical way, is a myth. As the New Testament scholar and specialist in pagan cosmology, Peter Jones has pointed out:

> Christians in the first century lived under a regime that continually tempted them to modify their beliefs and adapt their behaviour to a culture that didn't share their essential faith. Christians throughout history have been in similar social settings, in cultures and under governments that had no regard for Christian principles. Christians…are called by God in his Word to know the particular ideas that constitute the world's pattern of thinking and belief; in this way, we can both resist the Lie and make a statement of Truth that understands and exposes the Lie and offers the only true hope in the gospel. Ignorance of this will produce faith-destroying conformity and compromise.[10]

The apostle Paul, acutely aware of his need for courage in the face of seemingly insurmountable opposition in that pagan world of the first century, says in Ephesians 6:19–20:

> Pray also for me, that the message may be given to me when I open my mouth to make known with boldness the mystery of the gospel. For this I am an ambassador in chains. Pray that I might be bold enough in Him to speak as I should.

This is how we need to pray and speak again in our own time. Paul knew the power and mystery being made known by the proclamation of the gospel. And he knew he was Christ's ambassador—one who would suffer, and was even now in chains for his profession of the faith. He did not seek escape from persecution by compromising the

---

[9] See 1 Chronicles 12:32.
[10] Peter Jones, *The Other Worldview: Exposing Christianity's Greatest Threat* (Bellingham, WA: Kirkdale Press, 2015), 132.

message. He was not interested in going with the flow, in making the gospel more palatable to the ancient world, shaving off the rough edges so that it might be made more acceptable, more respectable, or more attractive to his pagan hearers. His request was simply for boldness to witness as he ought.

Likewise, we are not to take flight, but must fight in prayer for the courage we need to witness to the truth with boldness, as we *ought* to speak. We should be confident of being granted this grace, because the Lord Jesus reminds us of his total victory, "You will have suffering in this world. Be courageous! I have conquered the world" (John 16:33). We have only one person to fear in life and that is God himself. The world and all its powers have already been defeated at the cross, triumphed over in the resurrection, ascension and session of Christ. As such we dare not *not* speak. Woe to us if we do not preach the gospel in a wicked and perverse generation. In the sobering words often attributed to Dietrich Bonhoeffer, "Silence in the face of evil is itself evil. God will not hold us guiltless. Not to speak is to speak. Not to act is to act."

2

FAITH, WORLDVIEW AND GOSPEL WITNESS: FOUNDATIONS FOR APOLOGETICS

"I WILL ESTABLISH MY COVENANT WITH YOU, AND YOU SHALL KNOW THAT I AM THE LORD" (EZEKIEL 16:62 RSV).

POLITICAL RELIGION AND THE CHALLENGE OF WITNESS

Despite the untold miseries and inhumanities inflicted upon Western Europe, the former Soviet Union, China, North Korea and indeed the world by the totalitarian political religions of the twentieth century, we have seen in the previous chapter that Western philosophical consciousness still longs to realize the ancient religious dream of utopia—one autonomous humanity united in a planned, scientific-collectivist order.[1] The West's ongoing legal revolution,

---

[1] For a full discussion of the Utopian ground-motive of Western political philosophy, see Joseph Boot, *The Mission of God: A Manifesto of Hope for Society* (Toronto: Ezra Press & Wilberforce Publications, 2016), 157–188.

liberal-progressive education, media and entertainment industries, all testify to this abiding anti-historical and egalitarian pining.[2] Salvation by politics is the dominant and deeply-rooted cultural religion of our era, and it presses in on us at every turn. This ancient and yet modern worldview is grounded in a faith commitment to the *de facto* divinity of human will and reason.

The Russian writer and novelist Aleksandr Solzhenitsyn, who was imprisoned and tortured by the communist ideologues, well understood the cost of witnessing to the truth in the face of utopian cultural religion. His work morally impaled an entire political system as he called upon his people not to 'live by lies.' He invoked a simple choice, "Either truth or falsehood: towards spiritual independence or towards spiritual servitude."[3] In exile Solzhenitsyn approved the publication of his *Letter to Soviet Leaders* which denounced Marxism, called for political change and declared the Christian faith to be "the only living spiritual force capable of undertaking the spiritual healing of Russia."[4] He knew the gospel of Jesus to be the only solution to the wickedness and hubris of the gospel of man, which preached a false salvation by politics. In his Nobel Prize acceptance speech he said:

> In the Gospel it says, "You shall know the truth and the truth shall make you free." It is fascinating, astounding. What does this mean: It means that the path to freedom lies not in the fact that the parliament made a law of greater freedom today, but [rather] that you have to go *through the truth*.[5]

---

[2] By the term 'anti-historical' I mean the *regressive nature* of the utopian urge that has roots as far back as the account of Babel in Genesis 11. Utopian political religion works *against* God's norm for historical development in terms of his kingdom purposes. Just as reasoning can be logical or illogical, art can be beautiful or ugly, human action can be moral or immoral, court rulings can be just or unjust, financial developments can be economic or uneconomic, all in terms of God's established norms for those spheres of life, so man's cultural-historical development can be historical or unhistorical when related back to God's norms.

[3] Aleksandr Solzhenitsyn, cited in David Aikman, *One Word of Truth: A Portrait of Aleksandr Solzhenitsyn* (Virginia: The Trinity Forum, 1997), 32.

[4] Aikman, *One Word*, 32.

[5] Aikman, *One Word*, 35.

For biblical faith, Christ Jesus is THE TRUTH, not a mere aspect or part of it. To realize either truth or freedom we must go through our Creator and Redeemer who is the way, truth and life (John 14:6).

To republish the scriptural *gospel of the kingdom* which uncovers a *fundamental antithesis* (thereby denying a utopian oneness for autonomous man) in human thought and action centred in the heart and affecting the totality of man's life and being, including his political life, is no easy calling. The practical task of witnessing to the renewing power of the gospel in our time is not for the double-minded or faint of heart—indeed, Christians are rather called to purposefulness and courage, and in the face of every obstacle, we are above all called to faithfulness (2 Corinthians 5:8; Galatians 5:22; James 1:5–8). Solzhenitsyn suffered greatly for his clear witness in an absolutist age. Can we expect to share this same gospel message today without suffering? The biblical answer is that we cannot—suffering to some degree is an integral aspect of the call to witness to the kingdom of God (Matthew 10:22; John 15:18; 16:33). It means being willing to face rejection, ostracism, persecution and perhaps even death for the sake of Christ.

THE RISING CULT OF THE INDIVIDUAL

Due to the West's *secular public confession*—its credo of salvation by 'science' and politics with an egalitarian insistence on human autonomy—we live in increasingly intolerant climes where people are often suspicious, even derisive, of *transcendent* authority and exclusive 'religious' claims rooted in a given faith. This superciliousness comes loaded with many uncritical misunderstandings—namely, a failure to recognize that the critic of 'faith' is himself *never without a religious motivation* active within the faith aspect of human experience, affecting and determining the total direction of his life and thought. In reality, undergirding the critic's own faith is something temporal, something created, that is surreptitiously being absolutized and granted a religious ultimacy in place of the triune God—a divine *per se*.

Commonly, in our humanistic age, where man perceives himself to be the measure of all things, the going substitute divinity is the *autonomous individual*—though this theoretical and 'free' *individual* is typically found delegating his radical 'freedom' to the *collective* (man enlarged in the state as a substitute divinity). In short, today's dominant worldview is devoid of a *transcendent-personal* referent. As the French philosopher Chantal Delsol has noted concerning this modern temper:

> Against the various creeds—may all perish, as long as we have this hope or that faith—we affirm, *a contrario*, may all faith perish, as long as *man* does not perish. This affirmation itself *rests on a certitude*, that of the *value of man*...the primacy of the individual over any universal is the governing principle of late modernity.[6]

Such a governing principle, which denies any transcendent universal over humanity, is certainly a *religious* principle—a fundamental *belief* in the primacy, indeed ultimacy, of the human ego. This cult of the free individual—though paradoxically the idea of the free individual is an abstraction incorporated as *part-to-whole* in the modern egalitarian social order—is the veritable religion of our time. It is a certitude which epitomizes the secular faith of the West in its various permutations. But note, this philosophical judgment that man's autonomous thought and self-will are the *supreme value* is an inherently *religious valuation*—and one that cannot be coherently justified.

THE CHARACTER OF WORLD-VIEWING?

It is critically important to recognize the true *character* of these types of valuations in our culture because there is no one we might encounter in the process of witnessing to the gospel—whether they profess to be part of any specific 'organized religion' or not—who is not committed, consciously or unconsciously, to a religious valuation; a world- and life-view. That is to say, everyone's life is governed by a particular motive-force, an *ultimate ground or principle*, even if that principle is the destruction of all 'faiths' in the name of man and his will.

This observation opens up to us the reality that, while the vast majority of people get along just fine without *philosophy* as a theoretical discipline, nobody is without a *worldview*. A worldview is an inter-

---

[6] Chantal Delsol, *The Unlearned Lessons of the Twentieth Century: An Essay on Late Modernity*, trans. Robin Dick (Wilmington, DE: ISI Books, 2006), 154.

pretative outlook on reality, a confessional vision or perspective on life. It consists of an interconnected set of basic beliefs about things, resting in a foundational faith commitment. Like a pair of lenses, it is not something we normally *see* (i.e. examine), but rather *see with*. Usually a worldview is held intuitively, even unconsciously, based on a person's diverse experience which, however inadequate or inconsistent, is nonetheless making a claim to some kind of knowledge—it need not have been theoretically accounted for to qualify as a worldview. A worldview is something held by all mature adults because each of us needs a creed for living—pure arbitrariness is intolerable to us.

It should be added here that in the scriptural view, there is an even deeper motivating force within people than the beliefs inherent in their worldviews. At bottom there is an underlying *ethos* that dramatically informs their particular view of the world; a *faith orientation* grounded in the *condition of the heart*. Founded in this apostate or regenerate condition of the heart, various worldviews emerge upon which human philosophies are subsequently built.

THE NATURE OF FAITH AND THE MYTH OF REASON

The Bible teaches that because of our rebellious condition in a fallen world, our misdirected hearts cannot be relied upon to steer us toward the truth until they have been *regenerated* and transformed by God's grace. Indeed, God says through the prophet Jeremiah, "The heart is more deceitful than anything else, and incurable—who can understand it?" (Jeremiah 17:9). In the Christian view it is the condition of our heart—*the root-unity of human existence in its religious relation to God*—that finally informs our worldview and our philosophy, guiding our beliefs and actions (Genesis 6:5; Exodus 4:21; Psalm 119:11; Matthew 15:19).

Of course, a secular world typically denies that our spiritual condition, our faith and the worldview interwoven with it, is the *root* of our philosophical views or behaviour, preferring instead naturalistic sociological, economic, evolutionary or psychological explanations. However, while recognizing the inherent complexity of human thought and behaviour, Albert Wolters has made an important observation:

> The question is what constitutes the *overriding* and *decisive* factor in accounting for the pattern of human action. The way we answer that question depends on our view of the essential nature of human-kind: it is itself a matter of our worldview.[7]

In other words, all explanations of human thought and behaviour are themselves rooted in faith and a worldview. This further implies that the notion that we can ignore the ethos of the human heart, step out of our ethical and emotional lives, and set aside our deep-seated and often unexamined confessional vision to dispassionately and objectively evaluate the claims of Christ in the gospel, is at best naïve. And as the philosopher Thomas Morris has noted, "it is a complete and, unfortunately, common distortion of the human condition to think that what we see is altogether *independent* of what we do and how we feel."[8] These insights taken together make plain that our willing, doing, feeling, thinking and believing are integrally related to one another and characterized ultimately by the condition of our hearts before God—by our faith.

Given the role of our heart condition and faith orientation in shaping our worldview, the *nature of faith* needs further examination. The life of faith, in the biblical sense, actually *underlies* our specific beliefs rather than being the sum total of them—so our faith-life cannot be reduced to creedal statements, though these are an important expression of our faith. Faith is therefore not something that can be reduced to categories like 'rational' and 'irrational.' To put it in more technical language, faith is actually *supra-rational* in that it rises above the rational.

Consider the famous biblical statement about faith in the letter to the Hebrews: "Now faith is the reality of what is hoped for, the proof of what is not seen.... By faith we understand that the universe was created by God's command, so that what is seen has been made from things that are not visible" (Hebrews 11:1–3). We are told here that Christian faith constitutes a reality and proof ultimately grounded

---

7   Albert M. Wolters, *Creation Regained: Biblical Basics for a Reformational Worldview* (Grand Rapids, MI: Eerdmans, 2005), 6.

8   Thomas V. Morris, *Making Sense of it All: Pascal and the Meaning of Life* (Grand Rapids, MI: Eerdmans, 1992), 124

directly in the living and powerful Word of God. The full meaning and significance of this biblical statement cannot be reduced to a simple concept; my 'faith-understanding' of God's creative power described here exceeds my rational grasp. Moreover, my confidence in God as Creator cannot be reduced to a philosophical argument or creedal statement.

None of this is to say faith is non-rational or illogical, it simply denotes that faith *transcends* the reach of the rational categories in which our theoretical reasoning operates. It is not that faith is about believing in logical absurdities like square circles. Rather, faith recognizes that there are mysteries which surpass the full comprehension of our logical reasoning. In other words, while our worldview ought to be rational, faith itself is supra-rational—it rises above and goes before our belief systems and theoretical thoughts.

As such, our faith cannot be reduced to a *conclusion* at the *end* of a train of reasoning, because our faith is the motive-force operative at the *beginning* of our thinking—it is our starting point. This fact points us back to the root of our existence, the heart—the religious reality of the thinking "I." Just as a person cannot be reduced to their biological, social, economic, moral or logical functions, so faith cannot be reduced to the sum total of a person's particular beliefs. Faith is a matter that arises from the depth of a person's heart and so *precedes* and forms a foundation for specific worldviews.

Unfortunately, within our contemporary spiritual climate the critical role of faith and *heart-disposition* in the process of worldview formation and the development of philosophical perspectives too often goes unacknowledged or unrecognized. Since the falsely-labelled Enlightenment, a secularizing Western culture has been very much concerned with allegedly faith-neutral evidences, ideas or proofs of human 'reason,' paying scant attention to underlying religious motives of the heart.

The concept of 'reason,' often paired with 'science,' is invoked in modern thought to *justify* ultimate truth claims. But from a Christian standpoint, the Western concept of 'reason' inherited from ancient Greek thought—where the soul was a kind of *rational substance* participating in a *rational cosmos*—is nothing more than human understanding mythically absolutized as the principle and source of all truth. This absolutizing is usually done without adequately taking into consideration the faith-based assumptions and presuppositions involved in forming such a theory of knowledge and approach to reality—a perspective that has been called rationalism. Because of this uncritical attitude, rationalistic philosophical trends still deeply influence the Western university today and impact popular culture through aggressive religious movements like the new atheism and various secular societies, all of which claim to be non-religious.

For convenience and rhetorical advantage, in a supposedly faith-neutral pursuit of rational or scientific knowledge (especially for the purpose of political, technological and social 'progress'), the relevance of ethical heart motives and *pre-scientific*[9] beliefs are invariably ignored. Exposing this willful omission is very important for Christian witness because if an ostensibly faith-neutral and autonomous 'human reason' in a 'rational world' that is 'just there' is the key to all valid knowledge, then man alone becomes the fountainhead of all truth (that is, truth finds its foundation solely within man himself).

If this philosophy and the faith and worldview underlying it remains unexposed, secularism is granted a free pass to control and distort the whole discourse. This is why many fail to see that today's secular cultural vision is a far-reaching *religious conviction* that, ironically, but quite necessarily, cannot be justified by an appeal to reason alone. To claim that human 'reason' (which remember in the Christian view is simply the absolutization of human understanding in pagan thought) is the *ultimate ground* of truth and knowledge based on an exercise in 'pure reason,' is clearly to argue in a vicious flat circle since the validity and authority of human reason is *already being presupposed*. In the same way, to deny the validity of rational thought by a reasoned argument to support radical skepticism is equally self-defeating. This means that if you are a rationalist, for example,

---

9 By pre-theoretical or pre-scientific I mean beliefs that are not 'established' by an abstract act of reasoning (by opposing the logical aspect of thought to the non-logical aspects of reality to attempt to gain a better understanding of them). Pre-theoretical experience is what some call naïve experience. We hold to many beliefs that are not 'proved' by reasoned arguments or empirical experiments and we have practical knowledge and wisdom that *comes before* theoretical thought (hence pre-theoretical). Indeed, theoretical thought would not be possible without our ordinary experience to give it content. We must all *believe* certain things before we can have theories about the world.

your *faith and belief* in rationalism cannot *itself be rational* because it *goes before reason*. In fact, justifying confidence in human rationality is here seen to require a supra-rational appeal to God, because confidence in the faculty of human understanding is presupposed in all forms of argument! One cannot argue for or against it without assuming its validity.[10]

ROOTS AND RELIGION

Despite these things, because of an often blind adherence to secular worldviews, it is almost universally assumed in our culture that only beliefs rooted in specific claims about a personal God and *revelation* (i.e. *transcendence*) are actually 'religious.'[11] As such they are deemed largely inadmissible when addressing the significant questions of life in the 'real' world—especially anything to do with education, the arts and sciences or public life. This serious error has been inadvertently encouraged by modern Christians because they have taken the view that the teaching of Scripture is "basically a matter of theology and personal morality, a private sector labeled 'sacred' and 'religious,' marked off from the much broader range of human affairs labelled 'secular.'"[12] As a consequence Christianity is deemed 'religious' (as opposed to rational and scientific) and as such must be clearly separated from the state in its educational, political and legislative life.

By contrast, secular and other humanistic worldviews are now privileged by society and said to be 'rational' or 'scientific' (not 'religious' and therefore supposedly of greater weight and importance), since they originate in the autonomous thinking of man— that is, in the world of *immanence* philosophy.[13] The truth, however,

---

[10] See James R. Peters, *The Logic of the Heart: Augustine, Pascal and the Rationality of Faith* (Grand Rapids: Baker, 2009), 164.

[11] Both Hinduism and Buddhism have found a warm welcome in the West and are widely practiced in various forms in our secular culture because they are, in their final conclusions, philosophically indistinguishable from atheism—with no transcendent-personal and no historical revelation from God. With many of their cultural elements from the East expunged, we have seen the Hinduization of the West via the popular atheistic spiritualities of the East.

[12] Wolters, *Creation Regained*, 8

[13] I use this term to refer to all non-Christian philosophies which look for the ground and integration of reality *within* the created order. For the Christian faith, there is a transcendent creator above all things who is the ground of all existence and whose

is that different worldviews and philosophies have different views regarding what is rational as well as the nature and limits of scientific investigation. Thus, popular secularism today simply engages in endless question-begging when it presents itself as neutral, rational and non-religious.

The fundamental difference between the pure *immanence* philosophy of the secular and pagan order today and the *transcendence* philosophy of Christianity is that the former seeks to account for the temporal created order by reducing everything to some aspect or other of that temporal order, whereas the latter points to a creator-creature distinction and therefore to the *transcendent God* as the origin and final point of reference for all things—including human thought. These two worldviews are poles apart and they are *both* faiths—they are both religious.

Choosing between immanence religion and the transcendent God of Scripture is inescapable because everyone requires an *ultimate ground* as the basis of their thought and life. Clearly, that may be God or gods; a vague divinity concept; some *visible* or *invisible* quality or entity in the cosmos, in short, a foundational principle (be it God, reason, matter, numbers, evolution, energy etc.) by which the whole of reality can be *accounted for* and explained.

To illustrate, the atheist has a supra-rational faith commitment to the idea that there is no creator-God. This is *not* a conclusion arrived at by logical demonstration, it is a religious confession. The result is that something *inside* the universe must be invoked to explain and account for the *totality of reality*. Similarly, the agnostic has a supra-rational religious confession that we *cannot know* if there is a God. Consequently they are committed to the view that judgment must be suspended on the issue of God and may even construct a philosophy on that basis (skepticism). Likewise the Buddhist has a supra-rational faith commitment to the idea that, at bottom, *all reality is one* and the distinctions that emerge from that unity are ultimately an illusion—a view shared by ancient Greek thought. This is not the result of demonstration because rational demonstration

---

law provides the integration or meaning-coherence for the universe. Immanence philosophy by contrast is forced to absolutize some aspect of creation itself as a substitute for God.

would itself partake in the illusion of rational distinctions! Yet their worldview is rooted in this essential commitment, and various permutations of Buddhist philosophy have arisen as a result—we could go on. Whatever a person's faith may be, its *root or origin* is found beyond the physical, biological, social, rational, emotional, or any other aspects of our temporal experience, in an *existential commitment of the heart*—a supra-rational ultimate ground that constitutes a sense of certitude. This is why it is appropriate to call all worldviews 'religious' because religion is about the *ultimate ground* of life and thought. Philosophical systems find their root in a person's worldview, whether inconsistent and incoherent or not, and that worldview is in turn grounded in the faith commitments of their hearts. As such, it is indisputable that we are all inescapably religious beings and in the process of our witness, this reality should be graciously yet uncompromisingly uncovered.

FAITH AND WORLDVIEWS

As we seek to give faithful witness to the gospel in a context teeming with apostate religious ideas, the Christian must remain acutely aware that these various humanistic philosophies of life do not and cannot *prove* their ultimate presuppositions in the manner thought by the optimistic thinkers of the Enlightenment and post-Enlightenment period.[14] We should not be intimidated or silenced by the grandiose claims of cultural elites, nor be consigned to a 'religious fringe' by those who refuse to acknowledge or recognize the nature and depth of their religious apostasy.

We have clearly seen that all philosophies of life are rooted in religious worldviews and that every worldview is, by definition, pre-scientific and thus characterized by *faith*. As the Dutch philosopher Andree Troost has noted:

> Questions about the origin, unity and destination of life and the world and everything in them are questions that are always answered by a conscious or unconscious, Christian or non-Christian *faith...* [that] Ethos forms the starting point that is part of the structure of all human life. Ethos is active as an

---

[14] See Boot, *The Mission of God*, 457–494.

inspiring and direction-giving motive force, and it influences the entire practice of life, including the pursuit of science.[15]

Scriptural faith in the absolute, creative and redeeming Word of God categorically rejects the pretended autonomy of human thought—as though people's thinking and beliefs about the world could be religiously neutral, or an impartial 'reason' could function as an independent and infallible law unto itself. A consistently Christian apologetic will seek to reveal the *deeply religious roots* which not only lie beneath our own biblical understanding of reality, but which undergird all other worldviews. Wolters is helpful here when he clarifies:

> A worldview is a matter of the shared everyday experience of humankind, an inescapable component of all human knowing and as such it is non-scientific, or rather (since scientific knowledge is always dependent on the intuitive knowing of our everyday experience) *prescientific*, in nature. It belongs to an order of cognition more basic than that of science or theory. Just as aesthetics presupposes some innate sense of the beautiful and legal theory presupposes a fundamental notion of justice, so theology and philosophy presuppose a pretheoretical perspective on the world. They give a scientific elaboration of a *worldview*.[16]

Those theoretical elaborations will lead to either intelligible and coherent, or unintelligible and self-defeating, conclusions, which is where the hard and critical work of Christian apologetics is done (we will return to this theme later). So the battle is not 'faith versus reason,' or 'science versus the Bible,' as the secular mind would falsely characterize it. The contrast is ultimately between two religious worldviews confronting one another—one covenant-keeping, the other covenant-breaking.

We can therefore step out with confidence and courage as we engage in the task of gospel witness, knowing that biblical faith has

---

[15] Andree Troost, *What is Reformational Philosophy? An Introduction to the Cosmonomic Philosophy of Herman Dooyeweerd*, trans. Anthony Runia (Grand Rapids, MI: Paideia Press, 2012), 33.

[16] Wolters, *Creation Regained*, 10.

its reasons of which vain and empty 'reason' knows nothing. The *gift of faith* in Christ, the certitude of our hearts in the knowledge of God, is grounded in the work of the Holy Spirit, not the reach of our minds (Ephesians 2:8–10). Since our faith is not the gift of 'reason,' it cannot be undone by the vain arguments and empty philosophies of men. As R. J. Rushdoony notes in discussing the thought of Augustine and Cornelius Van Til, "no one can have true intellectual knowledge of God unless he first has faith and, accordingly, is morally in tune with God."[17]

The Christian attitude toward the triune God as the ultimate origin, and our trust in God's Word as the ground of our *worldview*, forms the bedrock of our witness. "A biblical worldview is simply an appeal to the believer to take the Bible and its teaching seriously for the totality of our civilization right now and not to relegate it to some optional area called 'religion.'"[18] The gospel to which we bear testimony is rooted in the core scriptural teaching of free divine creation; our original fellowship with the triune God; our fall into sin and ruin by rebellion against him; and our redemption and renewal in the person of Jesus Christ as we move toward the final consummation of his *kingdom* purposes in the power of the Holy Spirit.

In a faithful Christian perspective this *gospel of the kingdom*, which highlights the central antithesis between idolatry and true worship (rightly-directed or apostate faith in the heart), is the key to the real meaning of all human thought and the historical-cultural development of man as he has applied his faith to life and the world. Thus, the ultimate starting point for understanding every human being's relationship to Christ's kingdom is the *condition of the heart* before God. We cannot engage in truly effective witness if we fail to understand the significance of the heart as each person stands *coram deo* (before the face of God).

HEART RELIGION
The practical implication of all this is that in our witness to the truth of the gospel we are addressing and confronting, not merely human

---

[17] R. J. Rushdoony, *Van Til and the Limits of Reason* (Vallecito, CA: Ross House, 2013), 26.

[18] Wolters, *Creation Regained*, 9.

intellectual *artifacts*—that is, arguments or philosophies set up against the knowledge of God—but the *hearts* of men and women. This fact *must* inform our *practice* of witness. The *heart* is the biblical way of speaking about the centre, the root-unity of the human person, who is more than the sum of their parts, ideas or temporal experiences (1 Peter 3:4). Remember, when we reflect upon ourselves, we cannot reduce the human heart (the essence of who the 'I' or ego is) to any aspect of our experience of the empirical world or any abstract *concept* of theoretical thought, since the heart is *that by which* we think, reflect on and encounter all of these realities. The heart (the true self) somehow stands apart as the *precondition* of our experiencing anything. In an important sense the human heart appears *supra-temporal* (surpasses the constant change of temporal reality) insofar as it is the *concentration point* for all temporal experience, referring us back to God (Ecclesiastes 3:11). Somehow, we transcend ourselves as we reflect on the changing world and our own thought! Blaise Pascal urged, "Be humble, impotent reason! Be silent, feeble nature! Learn that *man infinitely transcends man*, hear from your master your true condition which is unknown to you. Listen to God."[19]

Lying at the very root of people's worldviews, eclectic spiritualities, ideas and lifestyles is this *matter of the heart*. For the heart—not the philosophy we elaborate or espouse—is the *essence* of who we truly are (Matthew 12:34). As the writer of Proverbs states it, "as water reflects the face, so the heart reflects the person (Proverbs 27:19)." The heart of a person, which governs everything about them, is not something to which we have *direct* access. The heart, as such (not the physical organ of course), cannot be the direct object of scientific study or philosophical analysis. Accordingly we are not in a position to act as final interpreter or judge over the hearts of men (1 Kings 8:39; 1 Chronicles 28:9; Proverbs 15:11; Jeremiah 17:10; Luke 16:15; Acts 1:24). We are able to examine appearances (or fruit) in people's lives, in both their thinking and living, but God alone has perfect access to the heart (1 Samuel 16:7) and stands in judgment over it.

Given that the unity which is a human being finds its focal point in the *heart* as the innermost depth of the human personality—an

---

[19] Blaise Pascal, cited in Morris, *Making Sense of it All*, 137.

ego standing in a fundamentally religious relation to God and his creation—then the religious heart is central to how we *form* our beliefs, *embrace* worldviews and *answer* ultimate questions. Remember, *unbelievers* are not *non*believers—their faith is simply placed elsewhere. For a start this insight will help us not to think of the apologetic task as simply overcoming people's arguments, outsmarting them or defeating them. We cannot treat people as though they are simply walking ideologies to be exposed and overthrown; a person cannot be reduced to their worldview and philosophy. As Herman Dooyeweerd has pointed out about the whole process of evangelization and the progress of God's kingdom:

> [The whole struggle] is not directed against our fellow-men, in whose sin we partake and whose guilt is ours and whom we should love as our neighbors. That struggle is directed against the spirit of darkness who dragged us all down with him in the apostasy from God, and who can only be resisted in the power of Christ.... As Christians we shall hate that spirit because of the love of God's creation in Christ Jesus.[20]

Our apologetic engagement is dealing with people and their apostasy—a rebellion in which all of us once shared. Our neighbours and friends are not political animals nor reason incarnate! They are *religious creatures* dragged down by sin and darkness. All of the unbeliever's life, and all of the Christian's life, *is religion*, not simply one aspect of it, or certain confessional or ceremonial 'religious' activities. When the scientist goes into the lab, the artist picks up a brush, the pastor enters the pulpit, the architect drafts an office tower or the judge enters the chamber, each person's actions, thoughts and intentions are shaped by their religious relation to God. As Willem Ouweneel has accurately summarized it:

> Religion is a matter of the whole Man, and thus of the kernel of his total existence, his heart. In virtue of his origin, Man, as a creature of God and as the image of God, has an intense bond

---

[20] Herman Dooyeweerd, cited in Evan Runner, *Walking in the Way of the Word: The Collected Writings of Evan Runner*, Vol. 2 (Grand Rapids, MI: Paideia Press, 2009), 298.

with his Creator and Sustainer and is totally oriented toward him, all the time. Whether he eats or sleeps, buys or sells, drives his car, or washes his laundry, does his daily work or prays and praises, he is always doing all these things as standing either before God (*coram Deo*) and in relationship with him, or in the case of apostate Man, with the false gods.[21]

The Lord Jesus affirms that *the heart* is indeed the *arche*[22] of man's being as he stands in this religious relation, directing all his thoughts and actions, "for from the heart come evil thoughts, murders, adulteries, sexual immoralities, thefts, false testimonies, blasphemies" (Matthew 15:19). The heart is therefore the true seat of submission and fellowship or *conscious resistance* to God in all its forms. It is where we experience the reality of guilt and alienation; and it is where we hear God's call to us so that we might have "our hearts sprinkled clean from an evil conscience" (Hebrews 10:22). When we witness to others, fundamentally, God is dealing with people's hearts, through us. Men and women *know* deep in their being they are in rebellion against their Maker. A person may throw up their arguments and objections to the gospel, but we must never forget that they do so in religious apostasy and know in their hearts that they are without excuse (Romans 1:20).

This scriptural understanding of the heart, with its inescapable implication that all of life is religion, has, as already suggested, far-reaching implications for understanding the non-Christian's life and thought—and how we go about witnessing to the truth of the gospel. As Christians we know it is by *believing in Christ* through the grace and power of the Holy Spirit that our hearts are transformed, leading us to true knowledge, understanding and wise living. This is a work of all-conquering grace in which the living Word of God (1 Peter 1:23) grants the gift of faith (Ephesians 2:8), bringing regeneration by the Holy Spirit (Titus 3:5) uncovering the eyes of our hearts to the truth (John 3:3). We also know that because of the sinful rebellion of man's heart, the task of gospel witness brings us into

---

[21] Willem J. Ouweneel, *Searching the Soul: An Introduction to Christian Psychology* (Grand Rapids, MI: Paideia Press, 2014), 49-50.
[22] A Greek term meaning 'source of action.'

the realm of a radical spiritual conflict with unbelief (false religion) in all its manifestations, as well as spiritual forces of darkness (Ephesians 6). Indeed, it is this spiritual conflict that comes to expression through the competing worldviews and philosophies that seek to undermine faith in Jesus Christ, opposing the knowledge of God (2 Corinthians 10:3–5).

APOLOGETIC IMPLICATIONS OF HEART RELIGION
Given the nature of true knowledge of God and of ourselves—faith-based knowledge that arises from a *transformed heart and mind*—faithful gospel witness has a distinct character. We should not, like the unbeliever, pretend to a rational autonomy as though we are dealing with ostensibly neutral or bare facts and self-evident concepts to demonstrate by 'reason' the *probability* of certain propositions about God—as though such arguments could make the claims of Christ on apostate man any more palatable or plausible. Rather, as Robert Knudsen suggests, "argument, whether that of Christian philosophy or apologetics, must be carried out on the *foundation of the truth of the gospel*, from which it must live and upon which it must reflect, and it must depend on the power of the Spirit."[23]

In other words, as we proclaim and defend the faith we do so not from *without*, as though we stand in neutral, independent religious space, but from *within* the commitments of our scriptural confession and worldview. We should make no pretense at neutrality and must never allow in our witness that the non-believer is religiously neutral either. It is only from within a candid commitment to the Christian worldview that we can remain faithful to Christ and find a coherent way to uncover both the failure and self-destructive character of non-Christian worldviews and philosophies, and also articulate the explanatory power and transforming grace found in Christ, the eternal, creating and redeeming Word.

To describe this approach another way, it means the apologetic task cannot, in theory or practice, operate above nor skirt around the central claims of the gospel as its ground and starting point. As Knudsen again points out:

---

[23] Robert D. Knudsen, *Roots and Branches: The Quest for Meaning and Truth in Modern Thought* (Grand Rapids, MI: Paideia Press, 2009), 105.

An apologetic must respect God's witness to Christ and Christ's witness to himself. Considering who Christ is, these are at bottom one and the same. We must take our stance…solidly within the framework of the Christian world- and life-view, but at the same time offer a rational defense of Christianity…. It also means that one must *challenge the presuppositions of unbelief.* Christian apologetics must challenge that which lies at the *foundation* of man's rebellion from God and his Word.[24]

The force and power of this God-honouring presuppositional approach is remarkable. For our goal is to show that finally, because of the internal antinomies in secular accounts of reality, "given anything that is meaningful—indeed, given anything at all—one can provide an account of the fact that it is possible only on the foundation of God's revelation in Jesus Christ, as witnessed by the Scriptures."[25] Which is to say, all that is, even the possibility of theoretical and pre-theoretical thought itself, is possible only on the presupposition of a full-orbed *Christian trinitarian theism.* "Any other starting point is inadequate; it will be unable to offer us a standpoint from which we can understand the world in its unity and diversity."[26]

Though apologetic engagement and worldview analysis stretches the mind, and certainly formal academic apologetics is not for everyone, our evangelistic task is to uncover the self-defeating character of unbelief. As we step out boldly in our witness to the gospel, we do so knowing that Scripture summons all people to seek God, even as it promises that, if they do so with sincere hearts, they shall find him (Jeremiah 29:13–14; Matthew 7:7; Acts 17:27–28; Hebrews 11:6). God is doing far more in people's hearts and lives than we can possibly appreciate and he is able to use our apologetic witness as a tool in his hand.

[24] Knudsen, *Roots and Branches*, 102–103. For a full demonstration of this argument see Boot, *The Mission of God*, 457–494 and Joseph Boot, *Why I Still Believe. Hint: It's the Only Way the World Makes Sense* (Grand Rapids: Baker Books, 2006).

[25] Knudsen, *Roots and Branches*, 103.

[26] Knudsen, *Root and Branches*, 103. For a full account of Christian apologetics that approaches the task in terms of exposing the underlying presuppositions of unbelief and their inadequacy (that is in a transcendental critique), see Boot, *The Mission of God*, 457–494. For a popular presentation of this argument for the non-believer see Boot, *Why I Still Believe.*

So in our method, rather than endorsing or abetting people's vain and fruitless quest for true knowledge and understanding via the myth of unbiased 'reason' (rationalism), a strict empiricism (religion of scientism), or a hermeneutic of doubt and suspicion—as though man's thought was a light of its own—we must show people Christ, the light of the world. The scriptures give us the *assurance* of finding truth and life in the person of Jesus. Here alone we discover the certitude of the biblical worldview, where faith leads to understanding and spiritual sight to new life. There is no religious neutrality for Christians or unbelievers. Christ-centred witness should be our only practice, because "the Word of the living God has come with its revealing light into our life, and *all human life*, whether men are aware of it or not, *is some kind of response to that Word.*"[27]

---

[27] Runner, *Walking in the Way of the Word*, 4.

3

CHRIST-CENTRED WITNESS: STRATEGIC CONSIDERATIONS

"THE TIME IS FULFILLED, AND THE KINGDOM OF GOD IS AT HAND; REPENT AND BELIEVE IN THE GOSPEL" (MARK 1:15 ESV).

CHRIST-CENTRED WITNESS RECOGNIZES THE SPIRITUAL CONFLICT

In the previous chapter we considered the centrality of the heart, the role of faith, and the critical place of worldviews in human life and thought—including the bearing of these matters on the task of evangelization. But having established the significance and inescapability of *worldviews* for human thinking, we should not be fooled into believing that our witness to the truth is merely an *intellectual* endeavour. The battle we are in is, at its root, spiritual. Though their presence may be disguised behind various idolatrous philosophies, our true conflict is against spiritual forces of darkness. Granted, the prince of the power of the air and his minions (Ephesians 2:2) are not visible to the human eye, but the inscripturated Word of God reveals that all Christians are constantly engaged in a cosmic spiritual struggle for the ultimate victory of Christ's kingdom in the world (Colossians 1:13). Nowhere is this battle more apparent in Christian experience than in the task of witnessing to the truth of the gospel.

The children of God have been caught up in this holy conflagration between light and darkness ever since Cain killed his brother Abel. Jesus himself taught us unequivocally about his own mission in this regard: "Now is the judgment of this world. Now the *ruler of this world* will be cast out" (John 12:31). And the apostle John likewise affirms, "The Son of God was revealed for this purpose: to destroy the Devil's works" (1 John 3:8). So as we think through the nature of our own witness to the kingdom we must be mindful that our battle is not being waged against our fellow human beings as such, but "against the rulers, against the authorities, against the powers of this dark world and against the spiritual forces of evil in the heavenly realms" (Ephesians 6:12 NIV). These spiritual forces inspire and establish key strongholds, and Paul tells us what they are:

> The weapons we fight with are not the weapons of the world. On the contrary, they have divine power to demolish strongholds. *We demolish arguments and every pretension that sets itself up against the knowledge of God*, and we take captive every thought to make it obedient to Christ (2 Corinthians 10:4–5 NIV, emphasis added)

Notice that we are not demolishing and defeating *people*, but rather those *arguments* and *pretensions* which set themselves up against the truth and knowledge of God. Holding this in focus will help keep our hearts and attitudes right towards our neighbour as we share the gospel and demolish the empty philosophies which hold them captive.

Faithful Christian witness is thus informed and energized by recognition of a fundamental conflict, an inescapable antithesis between what Augustine called the "City of God" and the "City of Man"—two spiritual roots and two forms of worship. These two cities (or spiritual seeds) have two ultimate principles, two kings and two destinies. One revolves around the love of self (sin), while the other elevates the love of God and neighbour (righteousness). And while practically it is all too easy to underestimate this biblical distinction because we do not want to be seen to divide people, we have already seen that the biblical teaching regarding creation, fall and redemption (i.e. the Christian worldview), while divisive, is the irreducible core of our faith and cannot be set aside without surrendering the gospel altogether. This biblical gospel will often be divisive and cause great offense, even when we take care to be gracious in our manner, because it confronts *spiritual darkness* (John 3:19–21), speaks to the *heart* (Matthew 15:19) and comes to the root of our *religious rebellion* against God (1 Corinthians 2:14). In every way it makes men self-conscious of the great *antithesis*, often provoking a strong or hostile reaction.

This gospel of God we declare is *power*, for his Word is living and active and sharper than a two-edged sword, able to penetrate to the depths of man's being (Hebrews 4:12). When this sword of God's Word pierces the heart of a rebel, it is painful and searching, and a great struggle often ensues. In a critical passage dealing with the cost of discipleship, Jesus employs the metaphor of a sword to highlight the divisive nature of the gospel of the kingdom, allegiance to which may separate even close relatives (Matthew 10:32–39). Christ-centred witness will not shy away from this spiritual conflict, fail to highlight the great antithesis between the two cities or neglect calling upon God in prayer to shatter our spiritual foe and deliver people from the domain of darkness into the kingdom of light.

CHRIST-CENTRED WITNESS CONFRONTS THE PROBLEM OF SIN

While our struggle is against spiritual forces of evil, it is also directed against the sin they encourage and inspire. Scripture is plain that while principalities and powers are significant and influential, the spiritual *root* of human rebellion against God is found, not in external forces, but with indwelling sin itself (Ezekiel 18:20; Romans 6:23; Ephesians 2:1). In the grip of sin, and captive to spiritual darkness (Luke 11:20–23), men will *suppress* the truth and invent a lie (Romans 1:18). Remarkably, basic to that lie is the denial that we *are* sinners who stand justly condemned under God's wrath (John 3:18,36). Indeed, one immediate problem Christians face today when we seek to share the gospel with our neighbours is the near absence of any honest recognition of the true nature of sin or its immediate impact on the heart and human understanding. Though the good news we declare is a wonderful message of cosmic redemption, freedom and deliverance, in the West's gleaming Tomorrowland, we may well ask if there is anything left to be delivered from. Theologian and philosopher Peter Kreeft discusses this particular challenge:

> In the past, the difficulty in accepting Christianity was its second point, salvation. Everyone in pre-modern societies knew sin was real, but many doubted salvation. Today it is the exact opposite: everybody is saved, but there is no sin to be saved from. Thus what originally came into the world as "good news" strikes the modern mind as bad news, as guilt-ridden, moralistic and "judgmental." For the modern mind is no longer "convinced of sin, of righteousness and of judgment" (John 16:8).[1]

Without a basic awareness and honest acknowledgment of our fallen human condition, there is no good news in the gospel message and consequently no real conflict between darkness and light, truth and falsehood, good and evil.

Nonetheless, in spite of human efforts to bury and ignore the reality of sin, the pain, alienation, guilt and confusion that continue to characterize human experience demonstrate that the Bible tells us the unvarnished truth about ourselves and our world. Our Lord's historical mission of redemption and reconciliation with God still offers a hope more real than any empty promise of human salvation through scientific progress or political revolution in the modern world. As such, we can only do people good when we faithfully seek to uncover their suppressed knowledge of God and his righteousness, and humbly expose their sinful condition before him.

Awakening that awareness in our culture involves challenging the ideas that seek to airbrush the depth of our sin from view. For example, we face increasing degrees of *moral relativism* today which consider right and wrong to be dependent on the individuals or cultures

---

[1]   Peter Kreeft, *Christianity for Modern Pagans: Pascal's Pensees Edited, Outlined, and Explained* (San Francisco: Ignatius Press, 1993), 26.

that endorse them. On this view there is no objective, trans-cultural moral law-order by which all people are held to account. 'Sin' is just a primitive taboo and a matter of social perspective.

Another cultural current which tracks alongside moral relativism is uncritical *religious pluralism*. This perspective aims to embrace all religious beliefs as equally valid and to deny any legitimate ground for judging between them since, in this view, they are all reduced to mere *historical phenomena*—that is, no ultimate truth claims finally escape immersion in the flux of historical change. This is the faith of *historicism* which concentrates all reality within the historical aspect of experience and robs people of any objective, *transcendent* truth. Both moral relativism and religious pluralism are actually just sophisticated ways of attempting to escape the reality of sin and deny our accountability before God; both seek to make idolatry and sin an illusion. Consequently, as a whole, Western culture now eschews moral responsibility even as it rebels against the Word of God, rejects redemption in Jesus Christ and asserts a radical autonomy (self-law). This fact of sin, grounded in the rejection of God's law-Word and its replacement with our own, must be confronted and exposed as we bear witness to the gospel. To fail to address the reality of sin is to deny we have a gospel to share at all.

CHRIST-CENTRED WITNESS REJECTS AUTONOMOUS STARTING POINTS FOR TRUTH

We find throughout history that men love to cloak their *denial of sin* within high-sounding arguments of empty philosophies (Colossians 2:8)—autonomous reasoning which originates with the word of the tempter, "Did God really say?" (Genesis 3:1). In the name of reason, man seeks to justify himself and find a basis for truth and knowledge without reference to God—in short, to be as God and know (i.e. define) good and evil for himself (Genesis 3:5). He then proceeds, not only to separate himself, but to try and separate all creation from the living God.

It was René Descartes in the seventeenth century who, perhaps not fully self-consciously, made a notorious clean break with the transcendent God, asserting the autonomy of theoretical thought, thus divorcing knowledge from God and his Word-revelation. He re-established ancient philosophical foundations upon which many after him would build, bringing us to today's point of moral crisis. Descartes had sought to establish certainty by doubting everything that could be psychologically doubted in order to reconstruct knowledge on supposedly indubitable foundations—the notion of the self-sufficient thinking subject, '*cogito, ergo, sum*' ('I think, therefore, I am'). It was Cartesian thinking which fueled the Enlightenment movement. Catholic theologian Hans Küng describes the result:

> With Descartes, European consciousness in a critical development reached an epochal turning point. Basic certainty is no longer centred on God, but on man. In other words, the medieval way of reasoning from certainty of God to certainty of the self is replaced by the modern approach: from certainty of the self to certainty of God.[2]

Descartes thus proved a perhaps inadvertent midwife in birthing our cultural moment of moral relativism, religious pluralism and widespread agnosticism. Following Descartes, what counts for truth today no longer seeks its ultimate foundation in God and his Word-revelation, but remains centred on the autonomous subject, deconstructing history, morality and everything else besides by means of a corrosive pride, sinful self-will and destructive doubt.

As heirs of this method, people today have gradually lost any real certainty, even with respect the nature of man himself—i.e. an understanding of 'what man is,' never mind who God is. This is an inevitable slide toward the abyss when the only authority acknowledged is the autonomous mind of man, individual or collective. Unsurprisingly, the result of this blind faith in our own independent thought has been disillusionment, confusion and increasing despair, especially among youth. Kreeft, in his book *Christianity for Modern Pagans*, compares this rebellious epistemological project of Descartes (and those in his line of thought) and its results with the Christ-centred approach of his Augustinian contemporary Blaise Pascal. Kreeft observes that Descartes sought certainty, utility and ease, while Pascal sought the kind of knowledge and understanding

---

[2] Hans Küng, *Does God Exist? An Answer for Today* (New York: Doubleday, 1978), 15.

that comes through faith in Jesus Christ:

> [Descartes'] chief critique of the ancients was that they lacked certainty, or "a sufficient criterion." Certainty, in turn, was his means to the end of utility, or efficiency, or "the conquest of nature." This technological conquest, in turn, was a means to the "relief of man's estate," that is, ease, comfort, the abolition of suffering. Yet these are precisely the three things his philosophy, and the civilization that has been seduced by it, not only fails to deliver but destroys. Life has never been so full of confusion and uncertainty. The average person has never felt so weak and helpless; and all social indicators show we feel exactly the opposite of ease and comfort.... Pascal is a prophet. Descartes is a false prophet.[3]

Küng agrees that Descartes had surrendered a truly scriptural perspective: "There is nothing specifically Christian about [Descartes'] philosophy: Jesus Christ does not appear to have played any part in it."[4] It was this that baffled the remarkable Pascal who, from the recounting of his conversion experience, to his apologetic witness in his Christian classic *Pensées*, testified to the power, centrality and indispensability of Jesus Christ and his inscripturated Word for true knowledge and understanding.

In view of the unscriptural nature and Christ-less character of Descartes' method, it is somewhat surprising to observe that many Christian apologists accepted and continue to accept the unbiblical presuppositions inherent within his approach. They too have tried to arrive at intellectual certitude and establish the 'idea of God' by building arguments based on the myth of an autonomous and neutral human reason. They implicitly or explicitly allow that there may or not be a God, so that we must 'go with them' to see where the 'self-evident' truths of 'reason' and 'brute facts' of experience lead us—as though human understanding, facts and experience are already intelligible without reference to the origin—to God and his Word-revelation in creation and Scripture. They fail to see that a

---

3   Kreeft, *Christianity for Modern Pagans*, 115.
4   Küng, *Does God Exist?*, 17.

brute fact is a mute fact. Since it is neither created nor related to any other fact by the plan and law-Word of God, it is impervious to interpretation—it is meaningless.

Because of this unscriptural tendency among rationalistic apologists (which remains the dominant approach with Christian apologetics today), some Christian thinkers have dismissed apologetics as redundant and finished, as though rationalism and the task of apologetics are inescapably involved in each other. As I have shown in an earlier chapter, this is not the case, and the opponents of apologetics have simply misunderstood the heart of the apologetic task, which is to give a faithful defense of the Christian philosophy of life based on the resources of God's self-revelation.[5]

In sum, faithful Christian witness must resist the temptation to flatter the natural man and his so-called 'reason' by rejecting an *autonomous* starting point for thought—that is, within thought itself as ultimate—and look to the transcendental starting point in Christ, the wisdom of God, as we pursue the task of evangelization and the defense of the faith.

CHRIST-CENTRED WITNESS HAS A CONFESSIONAL STARTING POINT FOR TRUTH

I have suggested that our defense of the faith goes wrong when it follows Descartes and grasps for truth and certitude by beginning with the autonomous self—the idea of self-sufficient reason—and therefore with doubt (mere probabilities). That is to say, our apologetics goes astray when it pretends to neutrality, is not pre-committed to Christ and side-steps a clear Christian *confession* in its method. Such a posture is not only unscriptural and lacking in both coherence and integrity, it reinforces the unbeliever in their rebellion and sin.

---

[5] This usually rests in a misunderstanding about the nature and project of biblical apologetics; it is not *optional* but a *scriptural* command to the church. The biblical call to "give a defense" and "persuade others" need not be party to the apostate Cartesian project. Rather, it can take a Trinitarian, Reformational and transcendental direction as exemplified in the work of Cornelius Van Til, Herman Dooyeweerd and John Frame. Furthermore, a narrative-based apologetic that seeks to capture the heart and mind with the epic of salvation—culminating in the incarnation, resurrection, ascension and session of Christ can be effectively employed within this transcendental paradigm.

The Christian evangelist and apologist should never forget that any method putting the reach of the rational faculty of sinful man in the place of final authority and judgment is making a huge faith commitment, and a highly destructive one.

So where can we find help and inspiration as we seek to confess and defend the faith with integrity? It is helpful to look to faithful apologists from the past who have been committed to a Christ-centred approach to the task. First, we should consider the creative process in apologetics as an art form; learning, reworking and redeploying the best insights and materials from past masters from times that are suggestive of our own. By grace we are historically situated at the head of a long line of faithful, fallible witnesses. Their message is our trust. The message we preach did not begin with us, nor do we have a right to reinvent it. Those who believe themselves to be so original that they wrap a new gift are not innovators but idolaters. As C. S. Lewis advises, "No man who bothers about originality will ever be original: whereas if you simply try to *tell the truth* (without caring two-pence about how often it has been told before) you will, nine times out of ten, become original without ever having noticed it."[6] In other words, telling the same truth faithfully makes Christian originality truly possible. Orthodoxy is not a black and white chalkboard that hinders creativity in communicating the gospel. It is a broad canvas and a full palette where one can find beautiful and colourful ways to communicate the unchanging faith of our fathers to each new generation.

This means, additionally, that the task of apologetics is not an exacting science in which we mechanically apply a particular methodology again and again to achieve the same result. Rather, it is a *craft* in which we learn to adjust our conversation and subject matter to fit different situations as we engage with diverse persons—all the while remaining faithful to Christ who is the Truth. In a science experiment, anyone given the same conditions, following the same method, can achieve the same result. But a craft is not like that and people are not like chemicals in a laboratory or equations on a white board. To practice a craft is to be guided by wisdom and a set of skills

---

[6] C. S. Lewis, *Mere Christianity* (New York: MacMillan, 1952), 190. Emphasis added.

handed down from one person to another, slowly mastering and being mastered by a knowledge that enables one to uniquely contribute to the craft as a whole.

In explaining and defending the truth of the gospel, Jesus was the master craftsman. He presented and taught the faith with all manner of creative arguments, stories, word-pictures and parables depending on who he was speaking with and their particular need, misunderstanding or objection. His divine eloquence and rhetoric were captivating. We must observe the example of Christ and the apostles and learn from the faith and strategy of faithful men who have gone before us, confessing and presenting the unchanging gospel in today's culture with all the integrity, skill, passion and creativity we can muster.

One such example well worth noting is that of St. Augustine. Augustine of Hippo lived, ministered and defended the faith at another critical turning point in history, during the fall of Rome (AD 410) and the transition from the ancient to the medieval era. In his day, as in ours, Christians and their faith were being blamed for the world's problems. They were regarded by many unbelievers as haters of humanity, while both paganism and various humanistic philosophies were very popular. In view of this remarkable similarity of circumstance, Augustine's faithful voice is both prophetic and instructive for our cultural moment. James Smith summarizes this church father's obvious applicability:

> There is a sense in which Augustine's cultural situation mirrors our own postmodern predicament.... Like Augustine we are constructing theology and engaging in Christian witness in the shadow of both a dominant empire and a religious pluralism. In short, for Augustine there is no secular, non-religious sphere as construed by modernity; there is only paganism or true worship.[7]

Augustine's peculiar relevance is illustrated powerfully for today's reader in both his *Confessions*, and his apologetic masterpiece, *City*

---

[7] James Smith, *Introducing Radical Orthodoxy: Mapping a Post-secular Theology* (Grand Rapids: Baker, 2004), 46–47.

of God. City of God is a *tour de force* of the kingdom of God, a cosmic narrative charting the histories of the city of darkness and light, the seeds of faith and disobedience, from the fall of the angels to his own time. Along the way he exposes the folly and vanity of pagan thought. In his *Confessions* Augustine moves seamlessly between personal testimony, philosophy, Scripture, prayer and praise—all the while centred in Christ and revealed knowledge of the triune God in the heart. His confession of the faith is integral to the totality of his life and thought. As Küng notes,

> Descartes' *Discours* and Augustine's *Confessions* are brilliant autobiographical justifications of each other's way of life. But we need to read only a few pages of either to sense a completely different mental atmosphere. Between them lies not only a millennium but a whole world.[8]

Like Augustine and those within this line of thought, as we respond to contemporary objections to our faith, we must remember that the truth of the gospel is not simply a *matrix of facts* or set of propositions to be accepted intellectually, but a relationship with a *person* to be received as Lord, by the heart, requiring the openness of one's entire being to God. This reality means that we cannot leave out the centrality of Christ and his Word in our defense of the faith. It is here the scriptural account of the kingdom and our confessional starting point become central to both the apologist and the inquirer knowing the truth as it should be known. As Küng again observes, "for both Augustine and Pascal, final existential certainty is rooted not in the 'cogito' of pure reason but in the 'credo' of the biblical message.... For [Augustine] what is decisive is *crede, ut intellegas,* 'believe in order to know.'"[9] If we do not follow this course, we will find ourselves using the same autonomous method as the world, which has proven wholly inadequate to arrive at the desired destination—the living God, redemption, truth and meaning (1 Corinthians 1:20–25). Alvin Plantinga recommends a similar confessional stance: "I say Christian philosophers should address these questions and topics

---

[8] Küng, *Does God Exist?*, 20.
[9] Küng, *Does God Exist?*, 66–67.

starting from the *Christian faith*, using all that they know, including Christian teachings."[10]

Christ-centred witness must therefore have an unashamedly *scriptural* and distinctively *Christian* foundation. Our confession, profession and justification of the faith must be consistent and integrally related to one another. This is because our whole philosophy of life must be Christocentric. Nothing is untouched by the biblical ground motive of the kingdom of Christ. It is not our thinking that is ever ultimate but God's truth in the Son of God, the Word of life. In this biblically grounded and Augustinian view,

> a "Christian philosophy" is therefore not grounded in thinking as such but is reflective self-interpretation of the Christian faith, especially in regard to God and the human soul. Consequently, *submission to divine authority is prior to all searching and researching*. It is understandable that in this view—as opposed to the Cartesian—the principle *credo, ut intelligam*, "I believe in order to understand" should be mainly stressed.[11]

Human thought only finds adequate foundation when it finds its place under God's authority. The story of human philosophy proves the futility of seeking an underpinning elsewhere—it always ends it skepticism and hopeless antinomies. But when we accept Christ as the Truth by faith, we find we have a consistent, coherent and intelligible worldview that 'hangs together' from beginning to end. God's Word-revelation both in creation and Scripture is an unbreakable unity. Scriptural Word-revelation includes the *republication* of God's creation revelation. As such they are interrelated and presuppose each other, so that taken separately cannot be adequately known or understood. It is therefore incoherent to try and establish our apologetic upon so-called 'natural reason,' or 'natural theology' with its supposedly religiously neutral arguments (deemed more acceptable to sinful man) as a stepping-stone before speaking of Christ and the gospel. Not only is this inherently contradictory—for if God is the

---

[10] Alvin Plantinga, "Augustinian Christian Philosophy," in *The Augustinian Tradition*, ed. Gareth B. Matthews (Berkley: University of California Press, 1999), 20.

[11] Küng, *Does God Exist?*, 68. Emphasis added.

creator and ruler of all things then there is no natural 'reason' independent of God and no fact or argument can ever be religiously neutral—but creation, properly understood, only declares the same God, reveals the same judgment and refers us to the same living Word as Scripture itself. Fallen people in rebellion against God will not find God's Word-revelation in creation any more palatable than his Word-revelation in Scripture. Thus, we must both pursue and defend the truth in terms of confident submission to God and his Word.

The testimony of Scripture is abundantly clear, that the world, by its wisdom "did not know God" (1 Corinthians 1:21). That is why, as Merrill Callaway says, "No matter how much we strive, we cannot know or reach [God] on our own, *within* the world system.... As long as humanity reasons in a vacuum, no matter how skilled its thinkers or how sophisticated the reasoning, human effort will fail."[12] However, by recovering the centrality of faith in Christ as *the Truth* in our defense of the gospel, we can face our unbelieving age with confidence, finding our way out of the humanistic quagmire. Otherwise, even with the best intentions, we will become inadvertent allies of secularism, paganism and the empty philosophies of men. We need a return to our biblical confession, to the transcendent, triune God made manifest in Jesus Christ as our criterion in both apologetic message and method.

CHRIST-CENTRED WITNESS WISELY AND HUMBLY CALLS PEOPLE TO SEEK GOD IN CHRIST

From this confessional starting point, how might we begin to call people in today's culture to *believe* in order that they may *understand*? Firstly, for those engaged in sharing and defending the faith, it is quickly apparent that the attitude of the messenger is as important as the message itself—in fact the messenger is an integral part of the message since we are Christ's new humanity and represent him as priests to an unbelieving world (1 Peter 2:9). Given that our task is to "take captive every thought to the obedience of Christ" (2 Corinthians 10:5), which is a combative metaphor, we need to be *wise as*

---

[12] Merrill Callaway, "Does Logic need Faith?" in *Journal of Creation* 20, no. 2 (2006): 126–27. For a full account of this remarkable mathematical proof of "incompleteness" showing the incapacity of a system to prove all its own axioms, see pp. 123–27.

serpents and gentle as doves (Matthew 10:16) as we engage with our fellow men and call upon them to seek God before the harvest is past, summer is ended and the days of God's patience are over (Jeremiah 8:20).

Wisdom is required (Proverbs 11:30) because Christian witness is oriented toward the ends of repentance and conversion (Acts 3:19–21; 17:30–31) which, though pursued in humility and surrender to the command of Christ, will often be perceived today as a hostile act—an act of rhetorical violence. This is owing to the fact that the gospel drives people out of the shelters they have built to shield themselves from God's claims upon them and calls them to throw down their arms and surrender to the Christ against whom, in their ignorance, they daily make war. We have already seen that the reality of the Fall makes people captive servants of sin and, according to the apostle James, *enemies* of God in their hearts (James 4:4). This reality necessitated Christ's coming to *defeat* the powers of darkness and then continue, through his people in history, to plunder Satan's stronghold and build his kingdom by the power of the Holy Spirit (Luke 11:21–23).

Understanding this formidable reality, we can exercise true humility, meekness and gentleness with the unbeliever. Knowing that the true enemy has *already been defeated*, we have nothing to prove that Christ has not already accomplished and made plain (Colossians 2:15). Practically, there are of course approaches to gospel-persuasion that are virtually doomed to fail before they begin. A hostile verbal attack (even if done with a quiet voice!), for example, will invariably either drive people away or erupt in non-productive and emotionally charged argument, achieving little or nothing. There are plenty of ways to engage a discussion partner that do not involve arrogance, hostility or an unwillingness to listen to the prospective convert's perspective. We have nothing to fear from listening carefully and then responding in a scripturally-rooted fashion to the real questions, objections or fears that a person has, rather than simply assuming we know what they need to hear and battering them with it.

Remember, if the common *root of unbelief* is a *heart condition*—not a lack of information, evidence or convincing arguments for the gospel; if it is not so much a problem of insufficient rational warrant for faith in God, but spiritual blindness and sinful unbelief hindering a person, then the heart and its deep attachment to cherished lies must be taken into account as we witness. According to Christ, those who truly seek will find. This means, ultimately, that the reason unbelievers do not embrace the gospel is that, given various excuses rooted in their sin, they are not genuinely seeking the truth which is in Christ Jesus. As Kreeft notes, "If we do not love the truth, we will not seek it. If we do not seek it, we will not find it. If we do not find it we will not know it. If we do not know it, we have failed our fundamental task in time, and quite likely also in eternity."[13] So our task is to encourage the unbeliever, in the power of the Holy Spirit, to become a true seeker, for the Word of God promises, "'You will seek Me and find Me when you search for Me with all your heart. I will be found by you'—this is the Lord's declaration" (Jeremiah 29:13–14; cf. Matthew 7:7–8)

We must also be mindful that the call of the gospel is life-transforming. The claims of Christ are total and leave out nothing (Luke 9:23; Colossians 1:15–20). They are profoundly personal, totally comprehensive and lifestyle-challenging. The gospel is fundamentally a call to reorient every aspect of one's life and thought to Christ as Lord. Thus, we are not coming to the unbeliever with an abstract hypothesis to be coolly weighed on unbiased scales with few implications for their lives. On the contrary, it is literally a *new birth* that is required. And so there is no neutrality with respect to Christ, no fence-sitting once he has stated his claims upon us (Matthew 12:30). Presenting the faith to the unbeliever is much more like bringing a marriage proposal than trying to market a house or an effort to change someone's politics, and so we should act accordingly. Through us Christ is inviting people *to be his bride*, the church, not to join him at a gym class to improve our fitness. Joining a gym is just one more thing. Coming to Christ changes absolutely everything and costs us everything (Luke 14:25–35)!

As we share this life-transforming gospel we are coming up against a person's cherished artifices, forged to escape God's claim upon them. In the midst of their rebellion people often become *disillusioned* because they have nurtured so many self-made *illusions*. As a result, when we face them with the Truth in Christ and further shatter

---

[13] Kreeft, *Christianity for Modern Pagans*, 217.

those chimeras, they are liable to be angry, upset and even afraid. What is more, the enemy of our souls seeks to entrench people in their illusions and embolden their resistance to the gospel. Because of these things a direct and assertive confrontation (though some-times necessary or unavoidable), *if born of our pride*—treating the unbelieving person primarily as an *opponent to be defeated* instead of a lost soul blinded by illusions and desperately in need of Christ's redeeming grace—is not only counterproductive, it is dishonouring to God and incongruent with the gospel. As my former colleague Ravi Zacharias often says, there is little point in cutting off someone's nose and then giving them a rose to smell! On this subject, Søren Kierkegaard has written with insight:

> There is nothing that requires such gentle handling as an illu-sion if one wishes to dispel it. If anything prompts the prospec-tive captive to set his will in opposition, all is lost. And this is what a direct attack achieves, and it implies moreover the presumption of requiring a man to make to another person, or in his presence, an admission which he can make most profit-ably to himself privately. This is what is achieved by the indirect method which, loving and serving the truth, arranges every-thing dialectically for the prospective captive, and then shyly withdraws (for love is always shy), so as not to witness the admission which he makes to himself alone before God—that he has lived hitherto in an illusion.... However, if I am disposed to plume myself on my greater understanding, it is because I am vain or proud, so that at bottom, instead of benefiting him, I want to be admired. But all true effort to help begins with self-humiliation.[14]

To arrange our presentation of the truth dialectically is real wis-dom and this was regularly Jesus' own method. In parables he often evocatively and suggestively arranges the truth of the kingdom of light (including the truth of his own identity) over against the lies of darkness and leaves people to draw their own conclusions (see Matt. 21:45; Luke 6:46-49; 8:5-8). In fact, he often healed somebody and

---

[14] Søren Kierkegaard, cited in Kreeft, *Christianity for Modern Pagans*, 40.

then quietly withdrew so as to let both the healed and the crowd take it in and make up their own minds. As our Lord often said, "he who has ears to hear, let him hear" (Matt. 11:15; Mark 4:9). As we witness to the truth of the gospel our aim is not to presumptuously present ourselves to people as their superiors and teachers, but rather as servants of God pointing to *the Teacher*.

This being the case, we should always be self-aware and vigilant about our *motives* whenever we enter apologetic discussion or discourse. Far too many people involved in apologetics seem more concerned with winning arguments than winning people. And some rationalistic *forms of argument* used by many apologists imply that if only the listener were as intelligent as they are or simply more rational, they would inevitably become Christians. Like bulls in a china shop and armed with their arsenal of evidences they appear more motivated to display their learning and defeat opposition than to reveal Christ. But it is humility before God and the Spirit of wisdom that will give us success, not a belligerent, presumptuous or know-it-all attitude. As C. S. Lewis, an apologist of singular gifting, poignantly reminds us in his poetic evening prayer:

From all my lame defeats and oh' much more
From all the victories that I seemed to score;
From cleverness shot forth on Thy behalf,
At which, while angels weep, the audience laugh;
From all my proofs of Thy divinity,
Thou, who wouldst give no sign, deliver me

Thoughts are but coins. Let me not trust, instead
Of Thee, their thin-worn image of Thy head
From all my thoughts, even from my thoughts of Thee,
O thou fair Silence, fall, and set me free.
Lord of the narrow gate and the needle's eye,
Take from me all my trumpery lest I die.[15]

If sinners are called to humble themselves before God, should they not see that attitude in the apologist also? For "the sacrifice pleasing

---

[15] C. S. Lewis, *Poems* (New York: Fount, 1994), 97–98.

to God is a broken spirit. God, You will not despise a broken and humbled heart" (Psalm 51:17).

Our true aim in evangelistic and apologetic witness is not to make the unbeliever listen finally to *us*, but rather help people be ready to listen to God and be taught by *him*. If listening to us were the end game, then battering people with argumentative, direct attacks might suffice. However, we do not use words simply for the sake of speaking. Rather, they are signs that call for a hushing of the restless heart, giving shape to the silence and mystery of Christ who speaks in a still, small voice. Our faith teaches us that *God reveals himself to people* in his good time, when they have been prepared in one way or another to meet him. Jesus was clear that "no one can come to me unless the Father who sent me draws him" (John 6:44). Thus an apologetic defense and explanation of the faith is *first* a matter of obedience for the Christian believer so that we might honour and glorify God and be strengthened in our own faith. And *second* it is a tool in the hands of our Lord and Master as he opens people's minds and renews hearts. We should never be deceived into thinking that it is our argument or creativity in itself which brings conviction or leads people to faith. It is God who both conceals and then reveals.

Indeed, God's self-revelation to man *presupposes* that in a certain sense, God is at first *concealed* from people with a particular condition of heart; there is no revealing without first a concealing. This concealing is a result of people's fallen condition and God's holy character. We all have a sickness of the inner eye that prevents us from taking in the brightness of Christ's light until the healing hand of grace restores our sight. Our Lord thus emphasizes that only those who are led to seek God find him, and further, that all those who truly seek him will certainly find him! These conditions for a true knowledge of God destroy the pretensions of the rationalist, who despises the humble search, while the promise nullifies the arrogance of the skeptic who despises the treasure and reward.

The *central problem* facing an unbeliever, then, is him or herself, not a lack of evidence or inadequacy of reasons to believe (Romans 8:5–8). As Christians we are certainly called and commanded to give a reason for our hope (1 Peter 3:15) and within the context of scriptural presuppositions offer our arguments and evidences—which rightly handled are truly powerful. But in their sins people tend to find only what they want to find and to see only what they want to see. As such we should not overestimate *our ability* to persuade, nor be discouraged when our best efforts are rejected or ignored. Because without grace men *suppress the truth* about God and exchange it for a lie (Romans 1:18, 25), the fallen human desire to escape our Maker and Judge is very strong. Reflecting this bizarre human malady, Gregory Benford, professor of plasma physics and astrophysics at the University of California, asks:

> Why is there scientific law at all? *I have a possible answer but as yet no proof of it.* We physicists explain the origin and structure of matter and energy but not the origin of the laws behind them. Does the idea of causation apply to where the laws themselves came from…? One can imagine a universe in which laws are not truly law-full. Talk of miracles does just this, invoking God to make things work. Physics aims to find the laws instead.[16]

In this desperate search to find the origin of laws Benford rightly rejects the religious hypothesis of an infinite number of universes containing an infinite number of law-orders (where our universe just happens, by chance, to contain this particular set of laws) as a counterintuitive let-off that explains nothing. Moreover, he recognizes our universe is fine-tuned and that law-order surely requires an ordering principle imposed upon reality. But the fact of creation as the concretization of God's Word, where law is an expression of the will of God, proves intolerable to Benford so he believes that prior intelligences (i.e. aliens) made other "smart" universes with the right fixed laws to produce ever grander structures. Notions of alien intelligences that evolved in some other reality and then created our universe is a more attractive faith for him than Christianity. The truth is, talk of miracles is not Benford's problem—the critical issue is, *who is performing them?* Naturalistic 'miracles' and a universe created by little green men are acceptable to him—the work of God is not. Despite his claims to the contrary there is nothing 'rational'

---

[16] Gregory Benford, "Gregory Benford," in *What we Believe but Cannot Prove: Today's Leading Thinkers on Science in the Age of Certainty*, ed. John Brockman (New York: Harper Perennial, 2006), 225.

or 'scientific' about Benford's faith commitment. It a religious confession by which he seeks escape from his Maker and Judge.

This manifestation of sin in humankind is seen again and again.
Fallen men and women do not want to meet God. Yet with amazing
audacity and hypocrisy they try to claim that their disinterest is
because biblical faith is irrational, or immoral, or unscientific, while
their faith is a rational, moral and scientific faith. C. S. Lewis is helpful in describing the unbeliever's insistence on an alternative divinity
concept—on a *divine per se*:

> Men are reluctant to pass over from the notion of an abstract
> and negative deity to the living God, I do not wonder…it is
> always shocking to meet life where we thought we were alone….
> An "impersonal God"—well and good. A subjective God of
> beauty, truth and goodness, inside our own heads, better still. A
> formless life force surging through us, a vast power which we
> can tap, best of all. But God Himself, alive, pulling at the other
> end of the cord, perhaps approaching at an infinite speed, the
> hunter, king, husband—that is quite another matter…. There
> comes a moment when people who have been dabbling in
> religions ["Man's search for God"!] suddenly draw back. Suppos-
> ing we really found him? We never meant it to come to that!
> Worse still supposing he had found us? So it is a sort of Rubicon.
> One goes across; or not. But if one does, there is no manner of
> security against miracles. One may be in for anything.[17]

No one can secure themselves against the living God breaking
into their lives, whatever they have been dabbling in, and this fact
should give us great confidence as we share the gospel. It is Christ
who comes to seek and save the lost and we are privileged to be his
ambassadors. Men will always be reluctant to 'pass over' from their
idol to the living God because the kingdom antithesis spans like a
chasm before them. But in his boundless grace God uses the humble
as instruments of reconciliation and redemption, granting us the
wisdom and boldness to speak the mystery of the gospel as we ought
(Ephesians 6:19).

---

[17] C. S. Lewis, *Miracles* (New York: Fount, 1974), 97–98.

CHRIST-CENTRED WITNESS TELLS
THE BEST STORY

In view of all that we have seen so far, the task of the Christian engaged in apologetics is to wisely, humbly and faithfully retell the Christian epic of the kingdom of God, manifest fully in the person of Jesus Christ and revealed in the Scriptures. Along the way we are to expose the antinomies, incoherence and inadequacy of alternative stories (accounts of reality) showing that the Christian worldview alone is able to give a satisfying account of life, thought and the intelligibility of human experience.[18] James Smith's comments here are instructive:

> Christianity offers a much better story. The mode of cultural engagement in the marketplace of ideas, then, is not syllogistic demonstration but narrative persuasion.... This narrative persuasion as a "new apologetic"...[points] to the mythical status of competing ontologies [theories of reality] and narratives and offers a counter-narrative from the Christian story that is embodied in practice.... *This does not negate the possibility of critique.*[19]

It is beyond the scope of the present discussion to demonstrate in detail how we go about an internal critique and examine the antinomies and incoherence of non-Christian thought, but in the following two chapters we will expose the mythic status of both the dominant worldview of the West, as well as the Islamic worldview, in order to illustrate the broad contours of our apologetic task and method. For now, our concern has been with biblical narrative persuasion, heart attitude and mental posture as we share the gospel—with unpacking and communicating the authority, beauty and power of the scriptural counter-narrative which unveils a true and better story, God's thesis!

The authority of our story (God's kingdom thesis over against the satanic antithesis) is carried within itself—which is to say, it is self-authenticating, because God's Word is power and authority; his Word *is Truth* (John 17:17). God and his Word are our final referent,

---

[18] See Boot, *The Mission of God*, 458.
[19] Smith, *Introducing Radical Orthodoxy*, 181–82. Emphasis added.

our *ultimate criterion* for truth—there is no appeal beyond them to an autonomous reason. It is not we who establish the authority of God's Word and the story of his kingdom in the earth. Authority has *been* established so that men will seek God with confidence and by faith have a heart prepared for understanding. Augustine tells us that the authority of the gospel narrative, has

> been brought about by divine providence through the utterances of the prophets, through the humanity and teaching of Christ, through the journeys of the apostles, through the derision, crosses, blood and death of the martyrs, through the exemplary lives of the saints, and in all cases, as appropriate for the time, through miracles befitting such great deeds and virtues. When therefore we see such great help from God, so productive and so beneficial; shall we hesitate to hide in the bosom of his church?[20]

Thus, in the biblical worldview, it is not men who *establish authority* by their 'reason,' it is Christ who is the source of all authority in heaven and earth. As such, the scriptural narrative presents Christ as the Truth—both as the *way* and as the *destination*. If Christ is only presented in our story as the destination of our search, while an autonomous 'reason' is put forward as the way to get there, we will actually end up arriving at a different destination, having distorted the biblical story. This is because the Christ who is acceptable to man's autonomous thought is not the Christ of Scripture.

Jesus Christ is not merely a *conclusion* at the end of an argument. He is the argument and the conclusion. Consequently, in faith, hope and love, we must urge those seeking the truth to pray, and to hear God's Word, as well as to read and reflect, so that by grace they may come to see Jesus for who he is—for nothing can be seen in its true light outside of the enlightening of Christ, "the true light that gives light to everyone" who came into the world (John 1:9).

---

[20] Augustine, "The Advantage of Believing," in *On Christian Belief: Augustine for the Twenty-First Century*, trans. Ray Kearney, ed. Boniface Ramsey (New York: New City Press, 2005), 146.

We have already seen that belief (a worldview) of some kind is inescapable and faith is a necessary aspect of life that is basic to all human experience. We all accept one story of reality or another. In other words, some kind of authority is a governing reality in *all* of our lives—the only question is which authority people surrender to. Christ established an unassailable authority for the Bible's account of reality as the incarnate Son of God, speaking to his creatures with truth and power, rising from the dead and ascending into heaven, now seated at the right hand of power (Mark 14:62). The Gospels reveal how Christ established authority through signs in word and deed, won followers with authority and continues to establish and make his church strong by our witness to the truth. Our faith promises certain fruit that is fulfilled in the believer and can be observed by the unbeliever. And so God has provided many convincing proofs (Acts 1:3) of the veracity of his kingdom for those who will seek with an open heart.

By embracing God's story in Scripture *by faith*, we are united to Christ in love. Through this fellowship he grants us a sure and certain hope (Hebrews 11:1); a knowledge and peace that transcends our theoretical thought and weak understanding (Philippians 4:7). Finally, the biblical story assures us our faith shall give way to sight, for "when He appears, we shall be like Him, for we shall see Him as He is" (1 John 3:2)—forever to be with our Lord, our Life, our Way, our End.

In all our evangelistic efforts and the constant struggle to defend our faith effectively with unbelievers, amid the many contemporary challenges hurled at Christians and as we war against our spiritual foe in heavenly places, we must remember that *the battle is the Lord's* (1 Samuel 17:47; 2 Chronicles 20:15; Revelation 16:14). Ultimately, the kingdom story and its impact in people's lives depends upon him. Without his power at work in us and within the world, convincing people of sin, righteousness and judgment, our efforts are ineffectual and feeble. If we do not depend upon Christ by the Holy Spirit; if we build upon any other foundation; if we rest on our arguments and abilities, we will utterly fail, for it is Christ alone who is the wisdom and power of God (1 Corinthians 1:22–25). Without love for Christ first and foremost, a love manifest in a life of faithful obedience to his Word, no matter how herculean our efforts, arguments and powers, we will be only a resounding gong or a clanging cymbal (1 Corinthians 13). But by walking in love and devotion to Christ as Lord, in spite of all opposition, *one word of truth shall outweigh the whole world.*[21]

[21] Alexandr Solzhenitsyn, "Nobel Lecture in Literature 1970," Nobel Prize, last modified 2014, http://www.nobelprize.org/nobel_prizes/literature/laureates/1970/solzhenitsyn-lecture.html.

4

UNCEASING OPPOSITION: BABYLON STRIKES BACK

HEAR, O ISRAEL: THE LORD OUR GOD, THE LORD IS ONE
(DEUTERONOMY 6:4 NIV).

So far in our study of the Christian's calling to witness to the truth
of the gospel, we have noted our cultural context in the West, dis-
cussed the significance of people's underlying faith and worldview
and considered the importance of a humble, Christ-centred and
respectful attitude in our approach to unbelievers. Critically, we have
established that all people are inescapably religious, irrespective of
whether they identify with a so-called organized religion. Religion
is a much more basic reality than participation in the specific rites
and rituals associated with personal or corporate acts of worship.
Rather, as Paul Tillich wrote with some insight, "Religion is the state
of being grasped by an ultimate concern, a concern which qualifies

all other concerns as preliminary and which itself contains the answer to the question of the meaning of our life."[1]

We turn now to those *ultimate concerns* and to the challenge of actually unmasking and critiquing worldviews competing with Christianity in the marketplace of ideas. The primary task for those engaged in Christian apologetics is to faithfully expose the origin, incoherence and finally the self-destructive character of non-Christian thought and highlight the antinomies patent in apostate religion and philosophy—directing people to Christ in the process. In our time, the dominant worldview underlying Western cultural life is humanistic and syncretistic. As part of our gospel witness, we will expose the ancient origins of this worldview, and point to its failure and inadequacy, while pointing toward Christ and his kingdom as the only satisfying answer to this apostate faith that has persisted from antiquity in various guises.

OPPOSITION TO GOSPEL WITNESS PROCLAIMS THE MYSTERY OF INIQUITY

Indicative of the popular spiritual syncretism of our age, I remember the publication in 2004 of a book by the former Anglican priest, Tom Harpur, called *The Pagan Christ: Recovering the Lost Light*. Its predictably Gnostic thesis was that *true* Christianity is really a beautiful ancient mystery cult that was grossly distorted by the early church because they deified a literal man, resulting in the alleged historical disaster of Western Christendom. The cure for history's ills, according to Harpur, is found in re-paganizing the world through a grand syncretistic mystery religion that will bring about world peace. For Harpur nature, not God in his Word-revelation, is our teacher and guide, so he laments that the exaltation of Christ in historic Christianity has undermined true spirituality:

> The church has too often let the divinity in every human heart—yours and mine—lie fallow...the deity that needs exaltation is that struggling "within the breasts of the sons and daughters of Earth. Jesus' enthronement is the disinheritance

---

[1] Paul Tillich, *Dynamics of Faith* (New York: Harper Perennial, 2001), 5.

of the common human being.... The historical Jesus blocks the way to the spiritual Christ in the chamber of the heart."[2]

Environmental neo-Marxism and evolutionary faith meet pagan spirituality in Harpur's eclectic and Oprah-style mystery cult. He makes emphatic claims for his pagan version of Christianity:

> While showing the deep relevance of the Jesus story, and the persona of Jesus for the life and spiritual growth of every Christian, this fresh view of the faith leads to an escape from the false religion involved in the current idolatrous cult of a "personal" Jesus. By showing him to have been deeply true in the mythical sense rather than literally as God, the vast theological offense currently given to the majority of other faiths, particularly Islam and Judaism, is not simply mitigated—it is entirely removed. Thus lies open a way to interfaith understanding that otherwise can never exist. This has enormous potential for world peace.[3]

He elsewhere explains his profound 'revelation' through the words of a friend, "I have discovered...I don't need an external, allegedly historical figure to experience God. But I do need the story of Jesus, the mythos, to bring home to me in power the meaning of the struggle and destiny of my own soul."[4] Leaving aside the fact that both Muslims and Jews believe Jesus was a real historical figure—thus rendering Harpur's claim that a mythical pagan Jesus would remove offense to other faiths absurd—Scripture is clear that such a heretical declaration is the very doctrine of anti-Christ and anathema. The apostle John wrote, "For many deceivers have gone out into the world, those who do not confess the coming of Jesus Christ in the flesh. Such a one is the deceiver and the antichrist" (2 John 1:7 ESV; cf. 1 John 4:2). In 1 John 2:22 the apostle states further, "Who is the liar but he who denies that Jesus is the Christ? This is the antichrist,

---

[2] Tom Harpur, *The Pagan Christ: Recovering the Lost Light* (Toronto: Thomas Allen, 2004), 176.

[3] Harpur, *The Pagan Christ*, 189.

[4] Harpur, *The Pagan Christ*, 176.

he who denies the Father and the Son" (ESV; cf. Galatians 1:8–9). Yet remarkably, neo-pagans like Harpur, often operating under the guise of Christianity, claim their Gnostic version of the faith is more authentic than that of Jesus' own disciples. For him, the Jesus story is nothing more than a morally inspiring spiritual allegory for the soul.[5] The gospel of Christ, for Harpur and for much of what passes for contemporary spirituality today, must be transcended by a return to a more 'ancient wisdom,' going back to the dawn of time that teaches a hidden secret. For,

> while literalist Christianism tends to rely on a supernatural... view of life and the universe, the ancient wisdom presented here as a matrix out of which true, spiritual Christianity emerged is entirely holistic and rooted in a natural reality that comprehends the entire cosmos.[6]

We immediately see in this 'mystery religion' that it is in fact *man*, as an aspect of nature, who is truly divine, and so it is really man and natural forces that are the objects of worship. Thus, for Harpur, Orion of the zodiac is the *real* heavenly Christ and the moon, every month, tells the story of our incarnation and ultimate resurrection (or 'recycling' in the grand circle of universal oneness).[7] We will return shortly to the world-unifying character of Orion, for this personage speaks to the ancient mystery of iniquity with its roots in Babylon (2 Thessalonians 2:7).

OPPOSITION TO GOSPEL WITNESS PURSUES SYNCRETISM

This illustration from popular religious literature published in the name of true Christianity (and this is just one among many such titles) goes some way to explaining why it is not uncommon in the West today to hear that there are many paths to God, many roads to enlightenment and many routes to spiritual fulfillment—this is the case even among many professing Christians. In fact, according to

---

5 Harpur, *The Pagan Christ*, 189.
6 Harpur, *The Pagan Christ*, 188.
7 Harpur, *The Pagan Christ*, 188.

the *Christian Post*, one in three professing evangelical millennials do not believe Jesus is the only way to God.[8] The emergent church movement, which is less a topic of conversation today, simply because it has become mainstream in Western Protestantism, preaches a religion-less and largely creedless Christianity, favouring 'social justice,' symbol, and esoteric experience that, in some circles, include prayers to God as mother.

Unsurprisingly, running parallel to this, we find that the modern Western state is keen to sponsor a vast freedom of worship (as opposed to true freedom of religion) and welcomes what it calls diversity, multiculturalism, toleration and the equal contributions of all religions to the tapestry of the social, cultural and political fabric. In short, there are many foundations for social order and many ways up the mountain of spiritual truth that supposedly *all lead to the top*—to God. The first obvious problem with such a conviction, however, is the pretended location of the observer of this religious phenomenon. Where would one need to be located to know that all paths going up a mountain lead to the top? The only location that would allow such a perspective is high above the mountain. So the humble assertion of modern religious syncretism amounts to an objective claim to an absolute divine perspective without the need for special revelation from the living God in Jesus Christ and his Word.

To put it another way, if all the beliefs, spiritualities and worldviews of the world are akin to blindfolded people all feeling a different part of an elephant and insisting that their description of what they feel is the true one—since one feels a tusk, another the trunk, another the tail etc.—then clearly all religions are in fact feeling the ONE divine truth, but from different perspectives. This would seem for some to establish the truth of religious pluralism or syncretism. But in what epistemic position does the teller of this story need to be? Clearly the religious syncretist believes he occupies a position of true objectivity, possessing absolute knowledge without any blindfold on! As such, this approach to religion not only dashes to pieces

---

[8] Stoyan Zaimov, "Only 1 in 3 Young Born-Again Evangelicals Believe Jesus is Only Way to Heaven, Apologist Says," *Christian Post* (October 12, 2013); http://www.christianpost.com/news/only-1-in-3-young-born-again-evangelicals-believe-jesus-is-only-way-to-heaven-apologist-says-106500/; accessed 06/04/2015.

the real and historical claims of biblical faith (and of other historical faiths) by relativizing them, but also presupposes an absolute, divine perspective on truth for the syncretist.

This pagan turn actually constitutes the basic claim of the West's humanistic religious pluralism—that man has a divine perspective *because he is an aspect of the divine*—and is implicit in all efforts at promoting *religious syncretism* which urge that we all 'just get along' and frowns upon evangelism. Inherent in this religious faith is a shift of the locus of revelation and authority from God to man. As the cultural theologian R. J. Rushdoony has put it:

> For humanism [paganism] man's *religious consciousness* and *man's psychology* is the real source of religious knowledge and revelation. The true word comes out of man, and therefore man's experience needs to be developed. Religion then ceases to be "Thus saith the Lord," the word of God, but rather becomes "Thus say I," the word according to man.[9]

This religious motive that has now deeply affected the church should not surprise us. Human beings, having been made in the image of God and in terms of his purpose, even when they rebel against God in religious revolution, cannot help but represent God's purpose, though now in a *deformed fashion*. As a result, humanity seeks to increase knowledge and establish authority for each area of life, but without the living God. Particular effort is put forward, since man is a religious creature, to find *religious unity* from out of man's collective religious consciousness as a prelude to socio-political unity apart from the Word of God—a counterfeit religious kingdom. However, true religion in biblical faith is God-centred and not man-centred. As Psalm 115:2–8 makes clear:

> Not to us, O LORD, not to us, but to your name give glory,
>   for the sake of your steadfast love and your faithfulness!
> Why should the nations say,
>   "Where is their God?"

---

9 R. J. Rushdoony, *Revolt Against Maturity* (Vallecito, CA: Ross House Books, 1987), 138.

Our God is in the heavens;
    he does all that he pleases.
Their idols are silver and gold,
    the work of human hands.
They have mouths, but do not speak;
    eyes, but do not see.
They have ears, but do not hear;
    noses, but do not smell.
They have hands, but do not feel;
    feet, but do not walk;
    and they do not make a sound in their throat.
Those who make them become like them;
    so do all who trust in them (ESV).

In the Christian view, the transcendent, *all-personal and all-relational* God speaks an infallible Word with binding authority, whereas in religious syncretism, the mind, idea or experience of man manifests the divine reality. The first view means concrete historical revelation in history, and the life, truth and community that comes from relationship with the living God. By contrast, humanistic, syncretistic religion leads to the lifeless, meaningless blankness described by the psalmist. Rushdoony has accurately described the dominant worldview of the West:

> In his religious quest, the humanist refuses to look beyond himself for his god. The more he intensifies his quest, the more he becomes like the idols described by the psalmist: *speechless, mindless and senseless.* Not surprisingly, the heart of mysticism… is the same speechless, mindless and senseless experience. The mystic calls for the exclusion of the external world, doctrine, revelation, and outer experience for total concentration on an inward blankness.[10]

If man speaks the authoritative word of truth, the new revelation, from his own consciousness, then he must also possess the power

---

[10] R. J. Rushdoony, "The Religion of Fallen Man," Chalcedon, last modified December 5, 2005, http://chalcedon.edu/research/articles/the-religion-of-fallen-man/.

within himself to fulfil that word. As such, interfaith, syncretistic advocates of today's humanistic religion typically believe that they can overcome war and hatred and inaugurate world peace through a new global religious order. This kind of radical pluralism and inclusivism, where human consciousness speaks the word of truth, has so invaded the contemporary church that many young evangelicals think that Gandhi, the Dalai Lama and Buddha have much to teach us about Christianity. In the rest of this chapter we trace the original source of today's resurgent paganism (which is the handmaiden of our culture's secular confession for the public space) and uncover its false pretensions. We will then contrast this religious syncretism and its social goals with the true unity that is found in the kingdom of God.

OPPOSITION TO GOSPEL WITNESS STANDS IN AXIOLOGICAL REBELLION

The syncretistic error begins with the radical assertion of *human autonomy*—the notion that man has an absolute freedom, is a law unto himself, and lives independent of God and his law-Word. Human autonomy is an *axiological rebellion*[11] because it is a rejection of God and his creation order—the true, good and beautiful as God has declared them—seeking instead to redefine good and evil in terms of man's own will and desire. As such, the recognition and exaltation of the triune God and his self-revelation in creation, in Christ and in Scripture, is seen as inhibiting man's true spirituality and the realization of his own divinity. However, this religious rebellion of man, as we have already seen, inescapably takes place *within* the framework of God's creational structures so that it is expressed in an attempt to establish, not only truth, but a great *community* or *kingdom* without God. This *requires* syncretism—a bringing together of the would-be gods into an organized community.

To better understand this apostasy we must go back to the original rebellion expressed in an ancient building project. From the beginning of creation God intended the establishment and development of a *holy society* or *city*, beginning with Adam and Eve, which, after the Fall, continued to be identified through the covenantal institu-

---

[11] Axiology concerns values and goodness, encompassing all moral questions.

tion of blood sacrifice, seen in Abel, Seth, Noah, Shem and Abraham. However, as Augustine argued, there was, in the providence of God, the parallel historical development of a *society of Satan* that was proclaimed after the building of a tower at Babel:

> Now the whole earth had one language and the same words. And as people migrated from the east, they found a plain in the land of Shinar and settled there. And they said to one another, "Come, let us make bricks, and burn them thoroughly." And they had brick for stone, and bitumen for mortar. Then they said, "Come, let us build ourselves a city and a tower with its top in the heavens, and let us make a name for ourselves, lest we be dispersed over the face of the whole earth." And the LORD came down to see the city and the tower, which the children of man had built. And the LORD said, "Behold, they are one people, and they have all one language, and this is only the beginning of what they will do. And nothing that they propose to do will now be impossible for them. Come, let us go down and there confuse their language, so that they may not understand one another's speech." So the LORD dispersed them from there over the face of all the earth, and they left off building the city. Therefore its name was called Babel, because there the LORD confused the language of all the earth. And from there the LORD dispersed them over the face of all the earth (Genesis 11:1–9 ESV).

Here, sinful man thought he could create an autonomous, religiously-united society centred in idolatry. This ancient religious project was an act of rebellion because it actually sought a closer unity of men *against God*. A great community thus settled in the area of Shinar, later known as Mesopotamia, and later again called Babylonia. The tower they constructed was almost certainly a stepped pyramid called a ziggurat. The top floor was likely used for astronomical and astrological purposes and as a centre for the rulers who had reached the highest degree of spiritual attainment in the mystery religion. With its top in the heavens, it was not intended to resemble a skyscraper but rather a *power centre equalling God* that probably sought to develop a new religious system involving the self-deification of men, by corrupting the meaning and purpose of the constellations, identifying them with spiritual beings and ancestors. It is of interest to note that the Bible tells us that the name *Babel* means *confusion*, whereas in the ancient Akkadian it means '*gate of god*' (*bab-ilu*); God's interpretation of the tower was different than apostate man's. By his own power, man was seeking to re-interpret all things and make himself the new god over the earth. True religion would henceforth be the product of *man's consciousness and self-deification*.

It is also noteworthy that the expression "let us make a name for ourselves" literally means to 'define, fix and establish' authority– a perversion of man's original calling to have dominion in the earth as God's vice-gerent; to name, categorize and bring out the order and potential inherent in God's creation. From Scripture we see that the apostasy of Babel was instituted in part for humanity to avoid being scattered, or separated in the earth, which for man implied division. From the beginning, equally important for humanistic and syncretistic religion was the idea that ultimate power cannot be a divided power, and so every effort was made to *compel human unity* in the name of the new faith in man's religious self-consciousness. In Genesis 11 we see that God's concern with this arrogant presumption was that, so united, man's dream of total power would mean an attempt at *total government and control*. Thus God undermined the idolatrous construction project and reduced them to confusion. Ever since Babel, a peculiar mark of judgment on all religious apostasy is spiritual, ethical and sexual confusion.

By way of contrast, in the biblical view, the unity of the human family was predicated on the *unity of God's own relational being and man's inward covenantal fellowship with God*, creating a geographically diverse community worshipping the living God. Abraham typified this faith, and the promise to his descendants was its outworking, ultimately in Christ (Galatians 3:16). Babel, on the other hand, was a heaven-defying project building a false outward unity by coercion; the fear of being scattered indicated the inward separation apostate man already felt from God. The Babylonian world-monarchy which followed was simply the dream of Babel continued. And so there stand *two views* of the Babel project in history. One sees it as a place of alienation and spiritual *confusion*, the other as the *gate of god*, resting on the satanic promise, "You shall be as gods." The tower was not only anti-god, it was an *indictment* of God.

Tellingly, this early period after the flood was perceived by many of the ancients as the re-birth of humankind, a kind of *second creation*. A leading British Egyptologist, David Rohl, has argued that Nimrod (later deified as the Mesopotamian hunter-god Ninurta) was the priest-king of Uruk, whose name derives from a Hebrew verb meaning 'to rebel.' Genesis 10:9-10 tells us that Nimrod, son of Cush, was a mighty hunter before the Lord and that he was a great empire-builder, beginning with Babel. According to Rohl, one of his first acts was to adopt the goddess *Inanna* as the patron deity of a great religious complex, the E-anna or 'house of heaven.' Inanna was a mountain goddess, ancient Sumer's favoured deity, because she represented fertility. Again, Rohl suggests she was the ancient *earth-mother goddess* who is recognizable as a deified Eve, "the mother of all living." The original home of this goddess was across the northern mountains in a Sumerian kingdom, a paradise land located in a place called *edin*—the Bible's Eden.[12] The Babylonians later called her *Ishtar* and the Canaanites *Astarte*. She is likewise the Ashtaroth of the Old Testament and the *Isis* of the Greeks. In an early form she was worshipped as the "lady of heaven" (possibly Virgo).

We know from Scripture and history that Nimrod was indeed the founder of the mightiest cities of the ancient world, and was divinized by later generations as, variously, *Marduk* of the Babylonians, *Osiris* of the Egyptians and *Ashur* of the Assyrians—the state deity. He was the founding father of *pagan priest-kingship* and thus *state worship*. He was adopted into the Western pantheon initially as *Ninus*; by the Phoenicians as *Adonis*; by the Greeks as *Dionysus* and by the Romans as *Bacchus*, and was often identified with the constellation *Orion*. Rohl goes so far as to argue that all goddess worship stems from the deification of Eve who is later made the consort of Marduk and that many of the male gods, including *Baal* (meaning Lord) of the Old Testament, are none other than a deified Nimrod, the first potentate on earth.[13] Ancient historian Bill Cooper largely concurs and argues that Nimrod was not only the most notorious man of the ancient world, but that he is the essential *founder of paganism* (humanistic

[12] David Rohl, *The Lost Testament: From Eden to Exile: the Five-Thousand Year History of the People of the Bible* (London: Century, 2002), 58–59.
[13] Rohl, *The Lost Testament*, 397.

syncretism), including the practices of magic arts, astrology, and human sacrifice—moreover, that he was deified and worshipped under numerous names from antiquity.[14]

One interesting and comprehensive work on this critical subject is that of Alexander Hislop in his classic, though controversial work, *The Two Babylons* (1858).[15] He identifies Cush (father of Nimrod) as the first ringleader of a corporate religious apostasy but also as Hermes or Mercury, for Hermes is an ancient Egyptian synonym for 'Son of Ham.' This would mean the first prophet of idolatry was Hermes (Cush) who fathered Nimrod, the great rebel and early empire builder. Hislop agrees with Rohl in identifying Nimrod with Ninus and as the builder of Nineveh. Hislop suggests that Nimrod's father was likely the founder of Babel and Babylon, while Nimrod was the heroic builder of them. Nimrod is then quickly deified and adored. Hislop writes, "Nimrod was the actual Father of the gods, as being the first of deified mortals."[16] He goes on to show in extensive detail that most of the gods down through the centuries, from various cultures, trace their genesis to Nimrod—from Hercules to Cupid, Kronos to Osiris, Bacchus to Orion, Krishna to Thor, they are all shown to be identified with the first great rebel Nimrod:

> A feature here, or an incident there, may have been borrowed from some succeeding hero; but it seems impossible to doubt that...Nimrod was the prototype, the grand original. The amazing extent of the worship of this man indicates something very extraordinary in his character.... Though by setting up as king, Nimrod invaded the patriarchal system and abridged the liberties of mankind, yet he was held by many to have conferred benefits upon them that amply indemnified them for the loss

---

[14] Bill Cooper, *After the Flood: The Early Post-Flood History of Europe Traced Back to Noah* (Chichester: New Wine Press, 1995), 189–190, 199.

[15] See Alexander Hislop, *The Two Babylons*, 2nd American ed. (Neptune, NJ: Loizeaux Brothers, 1959). It has since been demonstrated that Hislop exaggerated and even fabricated the connections between Nimrod and the Roman Catholic Church, including his identification of round communion wafers as images of the Egyptian sun-god Ra. I have no interest in defending his more tenuous or unsubstantiated claims, but simply in demonstrating the ancient provenance of pagan humanism.

[16] Hislop, *The Two Babylons*, 32.

of their liberties and covered him with glory and renown…for this very thing he seems to have gained, as one of the titles by which men delighted to honor him, the title of 'emancipator' or 'deliverer'…and hence in one form or another, this title was handed down to his deified successors as a title of honor. All tradition from the earliest time bears testimony to the apostasy of Nimrod.[17]

Notice, the deliverer is one who, by his apostasy, frees men from God. The adoration and devotion to this apostasy was ubiquitous. Orion, the giant and mighty hunter celebrated by Homer, is none other than Osiris and thus also rooted in Nimrod. It was held he was translated to heaven and added to the stars. Hislop's work not only reveals the traces of this same worship in the paganism of China and India, but shows that Nimrod was worshipped as a god because he was thought to be the woman's *promised seed*—*Zero-ashta*:

In almost all nations not only was a great god known under the name Zero or Zer, "the seed" and a great goddess under the name Ashta or Isha, "the woman;" but the great god Zero is frequently characterized by some epithet which implies he is 'the only One.' Now what can account for such names or epithets? Gen. 3:15 can account for them; nothing else can."[18]

In Genesis 3:15 the LORD says to the serpent, "I will put enmity between thee and the woman, and between thy seed and her seed; it shall bruise thy head, and thou shalt bruise his heel" (KJV). Zoroaster is certainly a mysterious ancient personage shrouded in myth and uncertainty, about whom there is little scholarly consensus[19]— there may even have been more than one person bearing this name, like the ancient Iranian prophet who made Zoroastrianism the dominant faith in ancient Persia. But it appears the original Zoroaster

---

[17] Hislop, *The Two Babylons*, 50, 52.

[18] Hislop, *The Two Babylons*, 59.

[19] The name Zoroaster was taken more than once by religious leaders. According to Pliny the Elder, there were two Zoroasters. The first lived thousands of years ago, while the second accompanied Xerxes I in the invasion of Greece in 480 BCE. Scholars generally believe that the first Zoroaster was a remote figure.

was the founder of the idolatrous system of Babylon and is therefore to be identified with Nimrod.

The traces of a primeval promise of deliverer are found in nearly all nations. Again, Hislop writes:

> There is hardly a people…on earth in whose mythology it is not shadowed forth. The Greeks represented their great god Apollo as slaying the serpent Pytho and Hercules as strangling serpents while yet in his cradle… the adversar[y] of the Egyptian god Horus is frequently figured under the form of a snake, whose head he is seen piercing with a spear. The same fable occurs in the religion of India where the malignant serpent Calyia is slain by Vishnu in his avatar Krishna; and the Scandinavian deity Thor was said to have bruised the head of the serpent with his mace.[20]

It seems evident from these various studies that the seedbed of all pagan religion, with its idolatrous sacrifices, secret symbols, astrological fatalism, orgies on the mountains, the deification of men and worship of state, kings, pharaohs and emperors, finds its genesis in Nimrod the great apostate. In his apostasy man decided he would bring about his own deliverance, restore paradise by his own power and deify his religious consciousness. The mystery of iniquity, Babylon the mother of harlots (Revelation 17:5), is the deification and worship of man in the place of God, and the original leader of corporate apostasy, the great prototype of man's own messianic claims, is readily seen in Nimrod, the rebel kingdom-builder.

The significance of this brief survey is to notice first, that the false gods in human history *are largely deifications of man's rebellious ancestors* conflated with spiritual powers and identified with the cosmos itself. Further, that the basis of all humanistic syncretism with its purported 'ancient wisdom' traces back to that infamous rebel Nimrod, who, given the common origin of all humanity and the confusion of languages at Babel, has gone by many different names since the beginning of human civilization. We shall return to the culmination of Nimrod's project later. However, it is crucial we

---

[20] Hislop, *The Two Babylons*, 60.

are aware that the historical genesis of today's religious pluralism and syncretism, with its *one-world religious objective*, is this original rebellion against God.

OPPOSITION TO GOSPEL WITNESS PRACTICES ONTOLOGICAL SUBVERSION

From this historic *axiological apostasy* of Babel proceeded an *ontological*[21] *subversion* of truth in the development and dissemination of *psychological religion*—man's idea, not revelation, asserted as the basis of truth. Now just as there is a correspondence between the mythological characters of antiquity and the historical original prototype (Nimrod), a study of ancient cosmology shows there is also a remarkable correlation between the *origin accounts* of the ancient world and their deities. Henry Morris observes:

> This remarkable similarity of the cosmogonies of many different nations of antiquity, as well as their respective pantheons of gods and goddesses, is obviously more than coincidence. The nations and their religious systems must have had a *common origin.*[22]

The ancient cosmogonies all begin with a universe *already in existence* in a formless or watery, empty state. Then the forces of nature, typically personified as gods and goddesses, act upon it. Given the historic global deluge and a cleansed earth emerging from the water, this phenomenon of a mythic watery, primeval beginning is not at all surprising. The ancient Greek poems of Hesiod and Homer have the gods and all creation evolving from primordial reality. In *Hesiod*, the undifferentiated natural world is simply "what is." Its existence is unconditional, giving rise to all else, generating a break between earth and heaven which is called "Chaos." Homer has a vast primordial expanse of watery stuff out of which evolve the gods and all material reality. Both accounts reveal a belief that the gods are *derivative*

---

[21] Ontology concerns being and the ultimate metaphysical foundations of life and thought.

[22] Henry Morris, *The Long War Against God: The History and Impact of the Creation/Evolution Conflict* (Green Forest, AR: Master Books, 2000), 235.

beings, and merely aspects of a more basic ultimate, unconditioned reality. This reality proves to be *nature* itself.

This same dependence is found in ancient Babylonian religious philosophy—a primeval chaos precedes and conditions the gods. Such gods bear no similarity at all to the God of the Bible. Werner Jaeger, commenting on Hesiod's poem "Theogony" (the genesis of the gods) writes:

> If we compare this Greek hypostasis of the world-creative *Eros* with that of the *Logos* in the Hebrew account of creation, we may observe a deep-lying difference in the outlook of the two peoples. The *Logos* is a substantialization of an intellectual property or power of God the Creator, who is stationed outside the world and brings that world into existence by his own personal fiat. The Greek gods are stationed *inside* the world; they are descended from heaven and earth…they are generated by the mighty power of Eros who likewise belongs within the worlds as an all-engendering primitive force. Thus they are already subject to what we should call natural law…. When Hesiod's thought at last gives way to truly philosophical thinking, the divine is sought *inside the world*.[23]

We know from Scripture, and it is agreed by many anthropologists, that all the nations and tribes do have a common origin. Moreover, the Greeks actually *acknowledged* that their religious philosophies were derived from the ancient Egyptians and Sumerians. The Greek and Roman pantheons have an almost *one-to-one correspondence* with each other and also with the Babylonians and Egyptians. Among these gods, the supreme Babylonian god was Marduk, who we have seen was almost certainly based on the personage of Nimrod.

Somehow then, this rebel man is also placed at the foundation of these pagan cosmologies, not just imperial history. It was the *Enuma Elish* myth (perhaps the oldest of the pagan myths) that was adapted by the later Greek philosophers for their own systems, first by Hesiod, then Thales and Anaximander. Thus, there in early Babylonia or

---

[23] Werner Jaeger, cited in John Lennox, *God's Undertaker: Has Science Buried God* (Oxford: Lion Hudson, 2007), 49.

Sumeria we may trace back to the prototype one-world religious leader Nimrod, that arch apostate, and to a people that gave us the foundational cosmogony upon which all the other origin myths of Rome, Greece and India have been constructed. While modern Western people do not typically speak of the gods, it is this ancient hope in the 'potential' and 'freedom' of human rebellion; faith in man's own mythic religious consciousness as the source of truth; and belief in a chaotic evolutionary past where creation emerged from cosmic dust and life crept out of the ocean, that is again flourishing and dominating Western culture. Its evil root is truly ancient—Babylon is striking back in our time.

Though the great origin myths of the world (with their gods) appear to have this common historical root, the *geography* of the myth is not the earth, but the heavens, and the actions are those of celestial bodies (principalities and powers both human and demonic). Pagan myths or mysteries thus passed on a body of astronomical and astrological knowledge.

The Bible clearly speaks of the mystery of "BABYLON THE GREAT, THE MOTHER OF HARLOTS AND ABOMINATIONS OF THE EARTH" (Revelation 17:5 KJV) from where we have seen the *entire complex* of pagan religion emerged. Man's rebellion therefore developed a *new religious ontology* that deteriorated from an original monotheism, into pantheism and polytheism and then into crude animism. There can be little doubt for the Christian who takes Scripture seriously that Nimrod himself (and those that followed his religious apostasy) was an occultist in communion with demonic spirits. More modern counterparts of the spirit of Nimrod, like one of the fathers of modern psychology in the twentieth century, Carl Jung, repackaged this occult psychological religion. Jung himself was deeply enthralled by pagan ontology and cosmology and was, by his own confession, introduced to his psychological ideas by demonic powers—he spoke in his 'Red Book' of his own spirit guide, Philemon, who had been with him for years.[24]

Leaving ancient history for the classical world of the New Testament, amid the religious syncretism of Athens, Paul's witness to the truth of the gospel was found antithetical to Epicurean and Stoic

---

[24] See Jones, *The Other Worldview*, 29–41.

philosophy with its inherited pantheon of ancient gods and pagan worldview. The Stoics, viewing all reality as pervaded by an intelligent divine force, were masters in the arts of divination—a practice common throughout the Greco-Roman world, linked to ancient astrological beliefs and tied to a pantheistic doctrine of fate. It is therefore inevitable that as we turn back toward a pagan worldview in our time, the occult arts are again being practiced widely in high and popular culture and in interfaith and, even ecumenical circles, prayers are again being offered to the goddess. In short, a wide variety of occult practices and various forms of goddess worship are very much back with us in a 'secular' culture. Moreover, and critically for our purposes, Richard Tarnas has pointed out:

> The existence of the world-governing reason has another important consequence for the Stoic. Because all human beings *shared in the divine Logos*, all were members of *a universal human community*, a brotherhood of mankind that constituted the World City, or *Cosmopolis*, and each individual was called upon to participate actively in the affairs of the world and thereby fulfil his duty to this great community.[25]

Here we see the socio-political vision of Nimrod for a world-community or kingdom constituted of an essentially 'divine' humanity governed by human 'reason.' As the primitive expressions of this humanistic nature religion in the ancient world gave way to more philosophical expressions of the same faith—like the form-matter scheme of the Greek philosophers (which retained a place for the gods as personified ideals)—the implications of their religious assumptions regarding the *origin* of all things (their divinity concept) became more self-consciously worked out. For example, Anthony Kenny has pointed to the culmination of the philosophical theology of the classical world in the Greek philosopher Plotinus and his abstract vision of the ONE—the One, Spirit and Soul. This unholy trinity is not made up of equal, relational persons like the triune God of Scripture, but constitute *emanations of the One* essence which is

---

[25] Richard Tarnas, *The Passion of the Western Mind: Understanding the Ideas that have Shaped Our World View* (New York: Ballantine Books, 1993), 76.

utterly simple. Kenny writes:

> If the One is beyond being, it is also beyond knowledge. [quoting Plotinus] "Our awareness of it is not through science or understanding as with other intelligent objects, but by way of a presence superior to knowledge." Such awareness is a *mystical vision*...because the One is unknowable, it is also ineffable.... Plotinus elsewhere says that we cannot even call the One 'it' or say that it 'is'.... We have to conclude that there is only a single soul...thus at the end of our journey we reach the One and only One.[26]

This 'Western' conclusion in philosophy reveals a remarkable similarity to the religious conclusions of the East. Philosopher Roy Clouser has pointed out:

> In Hinduism the divine (Brahman-Atman) is not considered a being at all. It is instead an indefinite "being-ness," or "being itself." For this same reason Brahman-Atman cannot be strictly called a god, if a god is taken to be an individual and personal. Buddhism also denies the divine is a being but goes even further. For fear that "being itself" is still too definite an expression, it insists on such terms as "Void," "Non-being," and "Nothingness" for the divine. So although these religions believe there is a divine reality, they do not believe the divine is a being at all, let alone a supreme one. [27]

These confessions are simply *philosophical expressions* of the empty, lifeless and dumb idols of Psalm 115 where man, stirred by the demonic realm, worships his own art—images of himself or beasts as gods. The philosophical idol of an original oneness, of an ultimate and essential unity to all things which lies behind all forms of syncretism, manifests the essence of the epistemological problem

---

[26] Anthony Kenny, *Ancient Philosophy: A New History of Ancient Philosophy*, vol. 1 (Oxford: Clarendon Press, 2006), 312–316.

[27] Roy A. Clouser, *The Myth of Religious Neutrality: An Essay on the Hidden Role of Religious Belief in Theories* (Notre Dame, IN: University of Notre Dame Press, 2005), 12.

of what Peter Jones, a leading expert in pagan thought, has called Oneism—where all reality is ultimately one (i.e. soul or ineffable principle), one is all, and all is an expression of the divine. The problem is, how can predication, differentiation, defining or describing of anything be carried on meaningfully if everything is at bottom actually one? With a real subject-object relation destroyed, true knowledge becomes impossible and all distinctions, including logical ones, are made illusory.

God's Word-revelation reveals that a relational structure is required for true knowledge to find a starting point. Because the apostle John tells us the Word was "with God" and "was God" (John 1:1), we see that the triune God (Father, Son and Holy Spirit) is both supreme *subject* and *object* of knowledge—a dynamic mutual reciprocity from eternity, of the infinite and personal. The God of Scripture is not an unknowable, ineffable unity who cannot create nor speak, but the foundation and precondition of all intelligible experience. If all that is is ultimately one, a blank unity or principle, then there is no real subject-object relation in reality, and no starting point for knowledge. The triune God is the transcendent starting point for knowledge in any area of life or thought.

Despite the clear epistemological dead-end for pagan, syncretistic philosophy, these monistic ideas have gained tremendous power and currency in the modern West, as the culture has been gradually de-Christianized. For example, scientist and popular writer Chet Raymo, whom the renowned evolutionary scientist Stephen J. Gould endorsed as a "wise religious humanist," who is showing how to "heal the false and unnecessary rifts in our intellectual culture" by bridging the gap of scientific knowledge and religion, has written:

> The God of spiralling powers resides in nature beyond all metaphors, beyond all scriptures, beyond all "final theories." *It is the God whose history began with the first human* who experienced awe, contingency, fear...there encounter gape-jawed and silent, the God of birds and birth defects, trees and cancer, quarks and galaxies, earthquakes and supernovas—awesome, edifying, dreadful and good, more beautiful and more terrible than is

strictly necessary. Let it strike you dumb with worship and fear, beyond words, beyond logic. What is it? It is everything that is.[28]

This is the resurgent religion of Nimrod in our time where *nature personified is worshipped*—for god is everything that is! Ultimately it is man himself who is the new source of adoration here, being the product of a divine nature, since this god's history 'began' when man became self-conscious—such is the psychological religion of apostate man!

The ancient rebellion of Nimrod at Babel thus leads to a polytheistic and ultimately pantheistic theological and philosophical vision in history that is able to embrace all the 'gods' (man's psychological religion of self-deification) into a social order that has a *priestly function for man, incorporating him into the divine whole*. As a result, a new religious system of creation-worship (see Romans 1) developed, centring on man as an aspect of the divine. The animals, the stars and forces of nature are likewise seen as aspects of divine being, with celestial and demonic powers influencing and shaping the future. Thus, from the cosmogony of Babylon emerges the broad philosophical ontology of paganism as everything emerges from one primeval chaos in a great *continuity of being*. This is why for many of the Greeks, nature was eternal, consisting of form and matter which led Plotinus finally to his absolute form—the ineffable One.

OPPOSITION TO GOSPEL WITNESS FINDS ITS END IN POLITICAL TOTALITARIANISM

Religiously and philosophically, this apostate faith connected man with divinity and enabled him to claim divine status or sanction for his politico-religious empire-building that required an enforced unity. We see this claim clearly in Scripture in the Babylonian empire and the life of Nebuchadnezzar, who set up a great statue of himself as a *representation of divine power* and required all people to bow down in worship (see Daniel 3). This was also the philosophical and political atmosphere into which the early church was preaching the gospel, where the Roman imperial cult required worship of the emperor as a

---

[28] Chet Raymo, *Skeptics and True Believers: The Exhilarating Connection between Science and Religion* (Reading: Vintage, 1999), 214–16.

god. And this is increasingly the atmosphere we face again today where, absent the theological language, the modern state usurps the prerogatives of God and demands allegiance to its redefinition of truth, justice and human identity. The political corollary of this ontological subversion of the Word of God was not, and is not, toleration for covenant-keepers—in either the ancient, classical or modern world.

Ancient Babylon is geographically located in modern Iraq; however, Revelation identifies Babylon, "the great whore," not only with ancient Babylon and Rome, but also with Tyre, Jerusalem and every other nation and empire that dreams of dominion and religious unity apart from God. What Babylon stands for in Scripture is an *ideal of unity*, peace and brotherhood which *mimics the kingdom of God*, under a false concept of deliverance (counterfeit messianic ideal), tempting man with an imitation, and is therefore properly called a whore. Religious whoredom happens whenever people attempt to usurp the prerogatives of God and seek to define, find or know the foundational truth about reality (i.e. ultimate concerns) by sidestepping the triune God and his Word-revelation. Spiritual whoredom denies the fact of sin (and its noetic implications), the righteousness of God and his law, and thereby seeks to circumvent the necessary atonement for sin in Jesus Christ—the true divine shepherd-king and deliverer. It is completely logical, then, that all pluralist, syncretistic visions of unity will deny the lordship and redemptive program of Christ in the gospel while seeking to absorb all man's self-justifying psychological religious expressions into a broad definition of human spirituality.

We have noted that man's own route to the 'divine' in this view is not a surrender before the living God and entrance into the kingdom by repentance and faith, but is found instead via a *self-realization of the divine within*. Here, *I am the logos* (divine) and so all human problems and difficulties, including the burden of guilt and shame, are not due to sin, but are products of a bad environment, lack of psychological freedom and the false exaltation of that man Jesus Christ. As a result, the one thing that cannot be tolerated in this psychological and political religion is an *exclusivist biblical faith*. The ecumenical world of interfaith religious syncretism, as Tom Harpur's book adequately shows, has no place for biblical Christianity and the absolute claims of Christ, and so neither does its counterpart and sponsor, the modern pluralistic state. It therefore becomes necessary in the modern West for the pagan worldview to replace scriptural Christianity in order to build religious and social 'unity' in society. With each person effectively regarded as *an expression of the divine*, the subjective self is made the source of truth. And so to challenge someone's psychological reality with the gospel of Christ is heresy because it is fundamentally divisive—tolerance and relativity are thus *required* for the political order.

Following Nimrod, that ancient rebel still unwittingly adored by the masses, the religion rooted in human autonomy means there is finally *no right or wrong or truth and falsehood in any metaphysical and objective sense*. As such, society must be organized in such a way that rebel man is free to express the will of the god within through whatever spirituality, sexuality or identity he desires and will pray to whatever, god, spirit or goddess *expresses his inner being*. As Peter Jones has noted:

> In this great expanse of energy, divinity and truth, *no religion can claim exclusive truth*. Because orthodox Christianity commits this unpardonable sin, it is the major obstacle to the religious and social harmony of the planet. Religions must blend into a global, unified syncretism...the various creeds are interchangeable and spiritual experiences are in communion with the same occult reality.[29]

This statement reminds us that there is, and always has been, an alliance in pagan thought between psychological mystery religion and political life. Roman political pluralism was made possible by the universal spread of the Greek language and culture, the development of a large trade market, a growing sense of political unity for the human race, and a cultural openness to the spirituality of the East. The result was the emergence of a religious syncretism in Rome on a Babel-like scale. Though outwardly diverse in the melting pot of the Greco-Roman world, these cults came together in a grand *synthesis*, unified by the view that behind their religious ideas was the same divine spirit or principle.

---

[29] Peter Jones, *Spirit Wars: Pagan Revival in Christian America* (Escondido: Wine Press Publishing, 1998), 27.

A wide variety of gods were housed in the *same temple* in the classical world, which is why Paul found the temple in Athens filled with numerous idols—including an altar to the unknown god (Acts 17:16–34). Moreover, it was believed then, just as it is today, that this religious syncretism was the solution to accomplishing world peace. Jones has noted that the Emperor Valentinian in AD 384 proposed a policy of religious tolerance:

> We gaze at the same stars, the sky belongs to all, the same universe surrounds us. What difference does it make by whose wisdom someone seeks the truth? We cannot attain to *so great a mystery* by one road.[30]

Humanistic politics and pagan spirituality inescapably came together and are very much coming together again in our time. Political power, pantheistic metaphysics, occult spirituality and various expressions of 'alternate sexuality' merged in the Greco-Roman culture to make this pagan colossus seem essentially impregnable to the Christian message. Again, as Jones correctly notes, "totalitarian political power joined with a syncretistic, all-tolerant world religion to insist on religious peace."[31] But this peace was only possible if you conformed yourself to the governing religious orthodoxy of the state. Osiris and Isis were welcome, but Jesus Christ the Lord was not. Christian resistance was to be crushed and if necessary Christians stamped out as enemies of the priestly and saving state. This was the experience of the persecuted church in the early centuries.

OPPOSITION TO GOSPEL WITNESS WILL BOW TO THE TRUE DELIVERER AND PRIEST-KING

In view of this, it is interesting to note that the Hebrew commonwealth was unique in the ancient world in *divorcing priesthood and kingship* in human authority; these roles were only to be united ultimately in *Jesus Christ* (cf. Genesis 49:10; Numbers 3:10; Psalm 110:4). His coming shattered the pagan view of priest-kingship, because he

---

[30] Peter Jones, *Capturing the Pagan Mind: Paul's Blueprint for Thinking and Living in the New Global Culture* (Nashville: Broadman & Holman, 2003), 31.

[31] Jones, *Capturing the Pagan Mind*, 32.

alone, as both fully God and fully man, is the emancipator and true mediator between God and man. However, as seen first in Nimrod, the pagan king was viewed as the manifestation of divinity and a human god—the eternal and temporal (philosophically the ideal and the material) mingled in his office by the commingling of heavens (stars and planets as deified men) with earth. In Rome, Julius Caesar was the democratic champion, assuming divinity, and was honoured by the Greeks of Asia as the offspring of Mars and Venus—a saviour for the human race. Octavian likewise claimed to be the son of God. Augustus Caesar made the same claim in the time of the early church. For these men there was a continuity of all being, and *deification* was the height of that continuity. The power source of such political authority rested in their false claim to be able to control, order and govern outcomes and the future. The priestly realm of political power was thus the *kingdom of 'god' on earth.*

In Israel, by contrast, God was King (even when Israel introduced a monarchy), ruling from his heavenly sanctuary. The *Holy of Holies* was his throne room among the people and all the earth his dominion. The Christian gospel announced the arrival in history of the King of all kings in the person of Christ, who came preaching the kingdom of God, and the apostles declared this message openly in the face of a pagan order which understood the implications of Christ's claim to kingship (Acts 17:1–8; Philippians 2:5–11).

The Roman world tried to meet the challenge of the claims of Christ and his church in several ways: syncretism, extermination and a kind of denaturalization (meaning to destroy the quality of), where they were ready to grant 'freedom to worship' so long as the church recognized the ultimate right of the state to *permit* freedom. The erosion of religious freedom in the modern West is moving in this direction, where increasingly there is a freedom to worship, but not freedom *from* the state's interference in the life of the Christian and the church.

In our time, the dominant strategy of anti-Christianity is syncretism with denaturalization. This *interfaith* perspective, steadily *enforced* by the modern state, is necessary to destroy uncompromising allegiance to the living God and his revealed Word. The claim of *human autonomy* therefore invariably entails *political totalitarianism,* because by it man creates a rival theological order in rebellion against God's rule.

This pivot from a supposed personal autonomy to a totalitarian social order—where the state gradually swallows all other spheres of life in a parts-to-whole relationship—is inescapable where the faith of Nimrod prevails, because it lacks a true concept of *transcendence* (only found in Trinitarian Christianity). If man's soul is deified as *logos*, if man is essentially divinized through his psychological religion, the result is absolutism, because power and authority become purely *immanent concepts*. Nothing stands above man and his political will to bring him into judgment—there is no appeal beyond the state.

This is one of the antinomies present in the modern pluralist and syncretistic worldview. In the name of freedom and justice, liberty is *eaten up* by political authority; cultural and institutional diversity by enforced unity; individuality by homogenizing collectivity; in short, the many are swallowed by the one. Modern democratic *political* liberalism, devoid of Christ's lordship, is simply a development of *theological* liberalism, which is the offspring of the religion of Nimrod. As the West has abandoned the transcendent God in socio-cultural life, it has transferred sovereignty from God to man and so *democratized authority* as the basis of all political order. In this view, truth and right are merely a product of the *psychology of the people*, not what God has revealed in creation and Scripture. Liberty under God and his law is thus replaced by the liberty of 'nature' and the development of man's right to express total autonomy from God as manifest in the 'will of the people.'

Syncretism (found in all theological liberalism) separates the state from any obligation to God's theological order and in so doing reduces Christianity to little more than another private psychological preference to be expressed primarily as social justice or humanitarianism. Consequently, God's moral law is repealed in the name of 'human rights,' for Nimrod's religious order cannot allow the existence of a *higher law* to critique and undermine the state's implicit claims to divine prerogative. *Syncretism is the democratization of religion* and within it is man's assumption of divinity in the political order.

We are currently experiencing the phenomenon that *freedom for the individual* is only transitional in the religious revolution of the West, because the source of truth, law and authority is shifting quickly from the *transcendent* God to the state and its agencies as an *immanent god*, beyond which there can be no appeal. Here the rights of the people (collective) become *divine rights* and so political power becomes inescapably totalitarian. The new 'revelation' proclaimed by this new god in our society declares that the family and church are traditional spheres of sovereignty which must be overcome, their authority set aside. Enforced *egalitarianism*, which is the political expression of syncretism, is the weapon of choice to accomplish this end. This suicidal social course emerges from and is entailed within the religious claim of *human autonomy*, revealing that *religious syncretism* and *political totalitarianism* are one.

OPPOSITION TO GOSPEL WITNESS IS SUBJECT TO THE CONQUEST OF CHRIST

It is important as Christians to be reminded, however, that because there is no other god but the Lord, the pretensions of Babel were destroyed by God himself. Scripture reminds the covenant people that Christ wins: "for of the increase of his government and peace, there will be no end" (Isaiah 9:7 NKJV), and "the earth shall be filled with the knowledge of the glory of the LORD as the waters cover the sea" (Habakkuk 2:14 KJV). There is only one potentate (1 Timothy 6:15), whose name is above every name, to whom every knee will bend in heaven and earth, the *true priest-king*, Jesus Christ, God's own Son. We have seen that pagan worship began with a kingdom vision—with Babel, Cush and Nimrod—a counterfeit human-divine king at its centre, arrogantly set in rebellion against God. This ancient conspiracy, with all its pretensions, is only a satanic imitation of the real kingdom of God, which shall prevail (Romans 8:37–39; Revelation 1:5-8).

Scripture makes plain that Jesus Christ was sent as covenant head of a new race that would build a new world (Romans 8:18–25; 2 Corinthians 5:17–20). In Adam, the original kingdom was lost through sin, but Christ, the second Adam, is building a kingdom that, as we see in Daniel's vision of the uncut stone, shatters the false syncretistic empires of men and spreads to fill the whole earth, a kingdom enduring forever (Daniel 2:44–45). Christ's death and resurrection introduced a new world that unmasked and smashed the powers of the old one. Certainly the conflict between his messianic kingdom and that of Nimrod rages as everything is shaken in the course of history, but the war is already won (Hebrews 12:26–29).

One critical event often overlooked in its significance in relation to the events of Babel was the giving of the Holy Spirit on the Day of Pentecost (Acts 2:1-41). This was not a narrowly 'religious event' giving a 'spiritual experience' to the disciples; it was a *change in the history of the world* as the Father and Son sent the Holy Spirit upon God's redeemed people to inaugurate the promises of a new covenant for the new creation. The immediate effect of this was the breaking of the curse of Babel. The curse on the *false unity* of Babel was *confusion*, so that they could no longer build the tower (and the apostate religious order it represented), for they could no longer understand each other. A shared meaning was lost and confusion was the result.

Amid today's supposedly unifying syncretistic worldview, it is ironic that men are everywhere in conflict and disunited—the breakdown of true community is all around us and the spirit of confusion prevails. The syncretism of Satan has always failed. But at Pentecost, when the Holy Spirit fell, people from all over the known world of various languages *all heard the gospel of the kingdom preached in their own language* as the apostles spoke in other tongues (Acts 2)! Here the true principle of unity was set forth by God; the communion of saints in the Holy Spirit as manifestation of the *kingdom of God* under the reign of the true priest-king and only potentate, Jesus Christ.

This pouring out of the Spirit created a new race of people from every nation—a new *family* of God. According to the gospel, no one can enter this kingdom without being born again into it by the Spirit of God (John 3:3–8). This reality rules out interfaith syncretism! To be part of this new world, the true *unity of the covenant people*, men must be born anew. The unity and peace that man craves with the divine and with all humanity because of his internal alienation from God, himself and others, can only be realized in a *covenantal oneness* with Jesus Christ and his fellow man by the ministry and grace of the Holy Spirit. In this fellowship, the true community, man no longer fears separateness or distinction as 'division,' for his internal alienation is done away with by the new birth. The new creation, the kingdom of God, is thus grounded, not in man's politics, but in the work of the Trinity, as the Father sends the Son for our redemption, and together they send the Spirit to bring us into covenantal oneness (not ontological oneness) with God and his people. The indwelling Spirit unites us in fellowship with God, shedding his love abroad in our hearts, creating a response of love in us. As Ralph Smith has described it:

> Through his indwelling, the Spirit unites God and man, bring-ing man into the covenantal fellowship of the Trinity…we could not be truly one with God unless we were made to be like Christ—not an ontological likeness, but an ethical one; *not a likeness that* eliminates individuality but a likeness in love by which our individuality is fully developed.[32]

When Jesus told us that his kingdom was near, he was referring to the restoration and glorification of the kingdom given to man at the beginning of creation, a kingdom he promised to build and extend, where Satan, his lie and all its expressions from Babel (the mother of all harlotry) to the present, would be overthrown and the kingdom restored to humanity in the Son of Man Jesus Christ. In short, man lost the kingdom in deep history, but in Christ the Lord, by the Spirit, he is getting it back! Christ's death and resurrection defeated our enemy, and as he now reconciles all things to himself (Colossians 1:19–20) in the process of time, his kingdom is being extended as he makes a new temple from living stones, ruling from the right hand of God (Luke 22:69). The prince of this age is cast out and his rule is passing away (1 Corinthians 2:6–8), for all power and authority in heaven and earth now belong to Christ (Matthew 28:18ff). And he sends us out as his witnesses to conquer in his name, in light of his unambiguous claim to kingship.

Our gospel witness is one that confronts and overthrows the false, satanic semblance of unity in the syncretism of false religion and offers instead the Kingdom of God, a covenant community of grace, enfolded in the loving embrace of the triune God. The intellectual antinomies, philosophical emptiness, spiritual bankruptcy, moral and sexual confusion of Babel, produce only broken lives and ruinous cultures, whereas the kingdom of God is righteousness, peace and joy in the Holy Spirit (Romans 14:17). It is this that the true Christian must preach and live. Only in this glorious hope can we confront

---

[32] Ralph. A Smith, *Trinity and Reality: An Introduction to the Christian Faith* (Moscow, ID: Canon Press, 2004), 144.

the broken Babel of our age and say with Paul, "Where is the wise? Where is the scribe? Where is the disputer of this age? Has not God made foolish the wisdom of this world?... The foolishness of God is wiser than men and the weakness of God is stronger than men" (1 Corinthians 1:20, 25 NKJV).

5

ISLAM AND GOSPEL WITNESS: CULTURAL RELIGION VERSUS BIBLICAL FAITH

FOR GOD DID NOT SEND HIS SON INTO THE WORLD TO CONDEMN THE WORLD, BUT IN ORDER THAT THE WORLD MIGHT BE SAVED THROUGH HIM. WHOEVER BELIEVES IN HIM IS NOT CONDEMNED, BUT WHOEVER DOES NOT BELIEVE IS CONDEMNED ALREADY, BECAUSE HE HAS NOT BELIEVED IN THE NAME OF THE ONLY SON OF GOD (JOHN 3:17–18 ESV).

So far we have seen that the culturally dominant worldview in the West at the present time is a humanistic, syncretistic, political faith that embraces a public secularity and pluralism undergirded by pagan religious assumptions. However, living alongside this failing belief system is a serious non-Christian competitor that has grown in strength and influence as the aggressive pluralistic ideology of our time has de-Christianized Western cultural life. While our social order is critically weakened by collapsing family life, falling birthrates, infertility problems and an inevitably crumbling welfare state—one that funds the abortion, sex-reassignment and assisted suicide of its population—an opportunistic Islam is seeking to take advantage of the historical moment.

And so we turn our attention to an internal critique of the *Islamic worldview*, unveiling the Muslim faith as a late, pseudo-Christian heresy. We will see that Islam is a socio-political religion which, though growing in the West, is a self-destructive ideology, riven with internal contradictions and antinomies, offering no lasting hope or coherent solution to the human problem. If Christians are to effectively witness to the truth of the gospel in our time, we must be equipped to unmask the pretensions of this resurgent faith. We must point both the Muslim, and the modern pluralist deceived by it, to Christ as the only answer to the religious and cultural longings of humankind.

RELIGION, WORLDVIEW AND THE CRISIS OF ISLAM

Twenty-five years ago, most people in our culture were unconcerned with Islam. It seemed remote, irrelevant and inconsequential to the majority of people living in Europe and North America. Few ordinary people had any substantive experience or acquaintance with its doctrines or cultural forms and most would have considered much of the Islamic world to be backward, largely poor, and, critically, *benign* as far as the West was concerned. That situation has been radically altered. The ideas, practices and ambitions of the Islamic world have found their way to the heart of Western Europe with large-scale immigration over the past thirty years, and high birth rates establishing populous Islamic communities in major cities. These communities are typically poorly-integrated with their host society, so that large metropolises in Western states have become essentially socially Islamic. As such, a once-familiar cultural landscape has been quickly and profoundly changed. Consider these remarkable examples of transformation in Europe: over eighty *Shari'ah* courts now operate in the UK—courts which have little regard, if not contempt, for British law. One of the most powerful and visible politicians in the UK, London's mayor, is an outspoken Muslim. Muhammad is now the number one name for new baby boys in the UK and Britain has become one of the world's most important centres of Islamic finance.[1] At this point, an astonishing one in ten people in the UK under the age of twenty-five are of Muslim faith. With this massive social shift has come the inevitable reality of *Islamic culture*. There are now thousands of mosques, Islamic centres and schools across Britain and Europe; in some places halal food is the only type of meat sold and served; Islamic banking is being offered by major financial institutions; and Britain is dealing with the highest female genital mutilation (FGM) levels in Europe.[2] The prisons and universities are becoming hotbeds for extremism and one in five Muslims in the UK have reported some level of sympathy for ISIS. Amsterdam, Rotterdam, Brussels, Marseilles, Bradford and Luton have Muslim populations of between 25 to 30 per cent and many more European cities have Muslim populations between 10 to 20 per cent.[3] Most obvious of all in recent years is the violent terror that has been unleashed across Europe, shocking naïve politicians and startling complacent and ignorant communities. The result is that many ordinary people are finally beginning to ask about the real nature of Islam. *What does Islam teach about truth and reality? Who was Muhammad? How did he live? What were his claims?* Can the Islamic ideology accommodate itself to Western society and pursue long-term peaceful co-existence in the West—a context that has historically enjoyed expansive freedoms and the rule of law, bequeathed by a Christian worldview? And for contemporary political life, can or will Islam adapt itself to the humanistic pluralism of our cultural elites?

Despite these vital questions, too few leaders are willing to speak openly and critically about the nature of Islamic thought and social order—its doctrines, cultural motives and objectives and its historic

---

[1] See Tim Dieppe, *What's Wrong with Islamic Finance?* (London: Christian Concern, 2016); http://www.christianconcern.com/sites/default/files/docs/islamicfinance_resource.pdf.

[2] "The Muslim Pound: Celebrating the Muslim Contribution to the UK Economy," Muslim Council of Britain; last modified 2013; http://www.mcb.org.uk/wp-content/uploads/2014/10/The-Muslim-Pound-FINAL.pdf.

[3] Pew Forum on Religion and Public Life, "The Future of the Global Muslim Population," *Pew Research Center*; last modified January 2011; http://www.pewforum.org/2011/01/27/the-future-of-the-global-muslim-population/.

incompatibility and therefore conflict with a Judaeo-Christian understanding of life and law. As a result, most people (including most Christians), are largely unaware that Islam is a total world and life view rooted in a particular concept of God and man, where the man Muhammad is the exclusive vehicle of true revelation, so that not just his ideas, but his precise manner of life, are to be followed in detail by the devout Muslim. Given that the life and character of a seventh-century nomadic trader and caravan raider from the Arabian desert is depicted as the *perfect example* of life to be followed, Islamic culture is imprisoned in paradigms and norms resistant to both critique and change. This obviously has significant implications for all aspects of future cultural development within Islam, as well as its relationship to western societies. As Gustave von Grunebaum has observed:

> It is essential to realize that Muslim civilization is a cultural entity that does not share our primary aspirations. It is not vitally interested in analytical self-understanding, and it is even less interested in the structural study of other cultures, either as an end in itself or as a means toward a clearer understanding of its own character and history.... The study of error and imperfection for their own sake does not deserve a supreme collective effort. The non-Muslim world is interesting enough, but, in a sense, obsolete, its foundations outmoded ever since the final revelation manifested through the Prophet the changeless norms of individual behaviour and social structure...this attitude leads to an extreme concern with power and success in history, or more precisely, with success in history as the *validation of revelation*—an outlook that represents the sharpest possible contrast with the outlook that governs Christianity's encounter with history.[4]

This incisive summary statement has far-reaching implications. Of particular significance is the contrast highlighted between the Christian and Islamic encounter with history. For much of biblical

---

[4] Gustave Von Grunebaum, *Modern Islam: The Search for Cultural Identity* (Westport, CT: Greenwood Press, 1962), 55–58.

history the progress of God's truth, his called-out people, and his redemptive covenant of grace appear to be halted—losing ground in the conflagration with sin, injustice and evil. Indeed, in the climactic moment of that conflict in the life of Christ, the cross initially appears a moment of total defeat—which is one of the reasons most Muslims deny that Jesus was ever crucified. Despite the physical resurrection, ascension and session of Jesus Christ, the Christian is called to take up their cross and follow him (Matthew 16:24–26), knowing and expecting that history will involve periods of suffering, exclusion, loss, decline and trial (1 John 3:13). In fact, seasons of hardship are basic to the social expectation of Christians because the biblical worldview teaches that sinful mankind is at enmity with God by nature, and is thereby hostile to those that represent him (Mark 13:13; Romans 8:7). As such, human nature needs to be renewed by grace (Ephesians 2:2). So while the Christian should labour humbly and faithfully in service to Christ in all cultural life, the historical results of that work are purely in the providential hands of God.

For Christianity, then, biblical revelation is neither validated nor refuted by periods of apparent defeat or success for the Christian religion in any given cultural moment. This is not so for the Muslim.[5] As the contemporary Indian Muslim thinker, Rashid Shaz, acknowledges, "We Muslims live with a paradox. If we are really the last chosen nation entrusted to lead the world till the end of time, why is it so that we are unable to arrest our own decline?"[6]

Moreover, because the *ground motive*[7] of Christianity is that of creation, Fall and redemption in Jesus Christ, a redemption of the *totality of creation* by the power of the Holy Spirit, unlike Islamic faith, it is of vital interest in Christian thought to understand all

---

5 Norman L. Geisler & Abdul Saleeb, *Answering Islam: The Crescent in the Light of the Cross* (Grand Rapids, MI: Baker, 1993), 160–161. This passage illustrates how certain victories in battle were considered divine confirmation of Muhammad's status and of God's favour, while interestingly, serious defeats were not interpreted as divine disfavour.

6 Rashid Shaz, cited in Robert R. Reilly, *The Closing of the Muslim Mind: How Intellectual Suicide Created the Modern Islamist Crisis* (Wilmington, DE: ISI Books, 2010), 159.

7 The term *ground motive* is used by the reformed, Dutch philosopher Herman Dooyeweerd to refer to the driving force, motive or core actuating idea at the root of any given worldview.

cultures, their history, philosophy and civilization. This is in order to gain a greater understanding of God's work in creation and history and to better appreciate the place of those cultures in the plans and purposes of God in the historical-cultural aspects of life. This knowledge adds not only to the Christian's self-understanding but also to his ability to witness with relevance and clarity concerning the gospel of the kingdom to others—especially with regard to how the redemption of Jesus Christ fulfils the religious longings inherent within all cultures and among all peoples. Furthermore, this attitude leads (and has always led) toward cultural development, growth and maturity, by taking and applying what is good and which conforms to God's Word-revelation and purpose from man's historical and cultural experience—wherever it may be found. This fundamental difference between the Christian worldview and that of Islam is foundational to an analysis of the *driving motive* within Islam and its cultural implications.

ACKNOWLEDGING THE ANTITHESIS

At first glance, people could be forgiven for thinking that Islam is basically like Christianity with a few superficial differences. After all, doesn't Islam teach belief in one God, in revelation, in marriage and family, in charity and justice, in heaven and hell? Let us examine these supposedly shared beliefs. *First*, it is true that both faiths speak about *God*, but on examination we discover that this word (*Allah* in Arabic) holds a totally different content for the Christian and the Muslim mind. For the Muslim, God is an unknowable monad[8] who does not reveal himself—he is essentially an *eternal will*, expressed in an eternal written text sent down in stages (Surah 43:2–4; 56:77–82; 76:23). As Robert Spencer notes, "For Muslims, the Qur'an is a perfect copy of the perfect, eternal book—the Mother of the book (*umm al-kitab*)—that has existed forever with Allah in paradise."[9] By contrast, for the Christian, God is a relational being, eternally existing as Father, Son and Holy Spirit, who is revealed clearly and truly

---

[8] A leading Muslim commentator, Beidhawi, suggests that the name Allah is derived from "an [invented] root *illaha* = to be in perplexity, because the mind is perplexed when it tries to form the idea of the infinite." See Geisler, *Answering Islam*, 14.

[9] Robert Spencer, *Did Muhammad Exist? An Inquiry into Islam's Obscure Origins* (Wilmington, DE: ISI Books, 2012), 126.

in the historical person of Jesus Christ, the incarnate Word of God. The gospels and letters of the New Testament are the historically-situated works of eyewitnesses, written under the inspiration of the Holy Spirit, which cohere completely with the inspired revelation of the historical patriarchs and prophets in the Old Testament. The human and historical element is never bypassed in the Christian understanding of God's self-revelation to man—indeed it is essential to it because God is a covenant-making God.

Second, the nuclear family (Christian marriage) is the fundamental social structure of Western civilization; the unity of marriage between one man and one woman as taught by Christ himself has been foundational to Christian society for centuries. By contrast, Islamic marriage is polygamous and is destructive of the unity, harmony and safety of the family. Ordinary Muslim men are permitted up to four wives, plus temporary 'wives' while on pilgrimage—although Muhammad allowed himself more. *Third*, both Christians and Muslims speak of charity, but unlike Christian charity directed toward all those in need and a fundamental aspect of Christian missionary history, Islamic charity is solely for the benefit of fellow Muslims, not the *kafir* (unbeliever). *Fourth*, it is true that both Christianity and Islam speak of prayer, but in Islam prayer is a matter of structured recitation five times a day to an unknowable god in the direction of Mecca, whereas in Christianity prayer is the interaction of a personal God with man in a covenantal relationship where neither form nor posture is imposed upon it to make it valid.

Fifth, both faiths speak of law and justice. But for Islam there is one law for the Muslim and another for the unbeliever (Surah 3:28; 4:144; 8:12). By way of contrast, in Christian society there is to be love for one's neighbour and equality for all before the same law rooted in the Ten Commandments (Exodus 12:49; Leviticus 19:34; 24:22; Matthew 5:44). This disparity is because Muhammad and Allah *hate the kafir* (Surah 9:29; 33:60; 83:34; 86:15), whereas the triune God of Scripture loves the world and came to seek and save sinners (Luke 19:10; John 3:16; Romans 5:6–8). *Sixth*, in Islam, any hope of paradise is based on the arbitrary will of Allah. Paradise is a libidinous eternal state that may or may not be attained by striving in the cause of Islam, whereas in the Christian faith, salvation is by the grace and love of God alone, by faith in Jesus Christ, who calls us

to follow him as his children and love one another (John 13:34–35).
Lastly, both religions are missionary faiths that seek to win converts,
but in Islam this is by almost any means, including killing, violence
and persecution, in order to bring the non-believer to submission (as
modelled by Muhammad himself, see Surah 9:29; 61:10). Whereas
in the Christian gospel, good news is preached so that people might
freely respond to it or reject it (Romans 10:14ff), and if Christ's witnesses and ambassadors suffer persecution as a result, they are to
love their enemies and do good to those that hate them (Luke 6:27ff).

These stark differences are basic to the persons at the centre of
their respective faiths. The true contrast between Islam and Christianity is between the persons of Jesus Christ and Muhammad.
Muhammad took up the sword to convert, tax or slay his enemies.[10]
Jesus Christ loved his enemies, forgave those who persecuted him
and went to the cross because of the great love of God and to win a
lost world by making atonement for our sin (1 John 2:2). In short, at
almost every point, while similar theological terms may be employed
by both faiths, their content is radically different.

No honest and effective witness can be made to the Muslim without a candid acknowledgement of the radically different starting
points we have—of the gulf that exists between the persons of Christ
and Muhammad. This fundamental antithesis is expressed in the fact
that the Islamic worldview always produces a radically different
culture and political system to that of Christianity—grounded in its
view of the *divine* and the foundations of *moral order*. If we care about
Muslims and our society, we will care about facing Islam honestly
and clearly in its varied implications. As Rebecca Bynum notes:

> We abandon our responsibility to our fellow human beings if
> we do not address Islam in all its aspects. As Ibn Warraq has
> noted many times, "Muslims are the first victims of Islam." And
> though Islam certainly provides a strong sense of belonging
> which benefits social cohesion it does so at the expense of
> personal freedom and individuality. Islam is something one is

---

[10] For a study of Islamic hostility and violence toward Jews and non-Muslims, see
Elias Al-Maqdisi and Sam Solomon, *Al-Yahud: The Eternal Islamic Enmity & the Jews*
(Charlottesville, VA: ANM Publishers, 2010).

born into and cannot leave without the most extreme intellectual, emotional and physical struggle.... The right to question and leave the religion one is born into, is a fundamental freedom absolutely denied by Islam.[11]

For those who would want to minimize the sharp differences between Christianity and Islam and naïvely or wilfully deny any fundamental cleavage in their understanding of God, revelation and salvation—suggesting instead that the starting point for engaging Islam should be an interfaith dialogue regarding supposed commonalities of faith (or shared beliefs)—we should bear in mind the clear teaching of Scripture. Here, truth is embodied in the *person of Jesus Christ, the second person of the Godhead* and exact imprint of God's nature (Hebrews 1:3), and there is no access to God except through him (John 1:1; 14:6). In clear contradiction to this non-negotiable element in the gospel, the Qur'an declares that there is *nothing like Allah*, and to suggest someone is made in the image of Allah is a blasphemy that denies God's nature (Surah 42:11). In short, for Islam, there is no image of God, no Son or any incarnation of the divine—for Allah is beyond being known. Islamic scholar Mark Beaumont points out:

> For the Qur'an commentator al-Tabari (d. 923) the naming of Jesus as God's son undermines the unity of God. By introducing concepts of fatherhood and sonship, Christians take away from God's true nature, since the Christian idea introduces a necessary connection between God and Jesus that reduces God's freedom and power.[12]

Muhammad himself considered the divine sonship of Jesus false prophecy (Surah 43:81), which recalls the words of the apostle John, "Who is the liar, if not the one who denies that Jesus is the Messiah? This one is the antichrist: the one who denies the Father and the Son. No one who denies the Son can have the Father; he who confesses

---

[11] Rebecca Bynum, *Allah is Dead: Why Islam is not a Religion* (Nashville, TN: New English Review Press, 2001), 120.

[12] Mark Beaumont, *Christology in Dialogue with Muslims: A Critical Analysis of Christian Presentations of Christ for Muslims from the Ninth and Twentieth Centuries* (Eugene, OR: Wipf & Stock, 2011), 8.

the Son has the Father as well" (1 John 2:22–23). For biblical faith, there is no true knowledge of God without the Son. But the Jesus (Isa) of the Qur'an is *not* the Son of God or the redeemer, nor is he the revelation and embodiment of truth. In Islam Jesus does not die at the cross to save sinners; is not resurrected from death; and came only for the purpose of foretelling the coming of Ahmad—another of the names of Muhammad, to whom Jesus will ultimately pay homage.[13] Thus at the most fundamental level—who God and Jesus Christ really are—biblical Christianity and Islam stand antithetic to each other. The cultural and social results that have flowed from that basic distinction can be seen in 1,400 years of history.

For there to be any meaningful beginning in understanding and witnessing to the Muslim as Christian evangelists, Islam must be recognized *first* as a totalizing worldview affecting every aspect of life and culture for its followers, and *second* as an ideology founded by a man who was concerned to set his teachings in antithetical relation, indeed opposition to, the triune God of Scripture and the gospel of Jesus Christ.

THE GROUND MOTIVE OF ISLAM AND ITS EARLY DOCTRINAL INFLUENCES

In our internal critique of Islam, we should begin by noting that the Islamic worldview is not entirely monolithic. There are various divisions, groups and sects within Islam, with differing claims regarding eschatology, spirituality, leadership succession from Muhammad (a source of endless Islamic conflict) and the immediate cultural implications of various Qur'anic teachings. There is, however, a *core of essentials* shared by the vast majority of Muslims today with respect to the Qur'an, Allah and Muhammad. While there are subtle doctrinal distinctions to be made between Islamic sects, it is possible to highlight the dominant direction of Islamic thought; to point to a foundational *ground motive* that actuates this influential ideology. What is the *religious* root from which Islam springs? I want to suggest that Islam is rooted in two fundamental ideas that are in a dialectical

---

[13] For a typically ill-informed Islamic dismissal of the New Testament record and claims of Christ by a moderate Islamic apologist, see Prof. Muhammad Tahir-ul-Qadri, *Islam and Christianity* (Lahore: Minhaj-ul-Quran, 2005).

tension with each other—*Nature* (fate) and *Revelation* (law). Both of these concepts point to a more basic and fundamental problem in Islam—its doctrine of God. To begin, then, we will consider the Islamic idea of *Allah*.

To understand the Islamic view of reality, of both *nature* (the world) and *revelation* (law), we must first consider the *divinity concept* of Islam because they are inescapably involved in each other. It is important to note that around the time of the birth of Islam in the Arabian Peninsula, the dominant religious ideas of the Arabs were pagan. Typically, paganism implies polytheistic *nature religions* that posit a mystical divinity concept (often indistinguishable from the totality of nature itself), combined with a pantheon of gods or spirits as emergent beings within nature, ritualistically involving both fetish and taboo (both of which are very present in modern Islam). Norman Geisler notes that the pre-Islamic religion of Arabia acknowledged a vague supreme being, "the Arabs of pre-Islamic days, despite all their idolatry, knew of and acknowledged Allah's existence as the supreme God."[14] Muhammad's own father bore the name Abd-Allah (slave of God), indicating that his contemporaries identified a supreme deity called *Allah*. As Zwemer argues:

> In pre-Islamic literature, Christian or pagan, *ilah* is used for any god and *Al-ilah* (contracted to Allah)…was the name of the supreme. Among the pagan Arabs this term denoted the chief god of their pantheon, the Kaaba, with its three-hundred-and-sixty idols.… As final evidence, we have the fact centuries before Muhammad the Arabian Kaaba, or temple at Mecca, was called Beit-Allah, the house of God.[15]

It is not easy to discern the exact nature of this supreme deity of pre-Islamic Arabia—even the origins of Islam itself are very vague and disputed—because of the variety of influences geographically. There is clearly a connection to astral religious beliefs which persists in the main symbol of Islam—the crescent.[16] Jacques Ryckmans has

---

[14] Geisler, *Answering Islam*, 15.

[15] Cited in Geisler, *Answering Islam*, 15–16.

[16] Jacques Ryckmans, "Arabian Religion," *Encyclopaedia Britannica*, last modified 2016; https://www.britannica.com/topic/Arabian-religion. "In Maʿīn the national god

also pointed out:

> Al-Ilāt or Allāt ("the Goddess"), was known to all pantheons. She is a daughter or a consort, depending on the region, of al-Lāh or Allāh ("the God"), Lord of the Kaābah in Mecca; he is also named in Thamūdic texts. Al-Ilāt formed a trio with the goddesses al-'Uzzā ("the Powerful") and Manāt (or Manawat, "Destiny"). Among the Nabataeans al-'Uzzā was assimilated to Venus and Aphrodite and was the consort of Kutbā'or al-Aktab ("the Scribe"; Mercury); among the Thamudaeans, however, she was assimilated to 'Attarsamay (or 'Attarsam). Manāt was depicted as Nemesis in the Nabataean iconography. The three goddesses were called the "Daughters of Allāh" in pre-Islāmic Mecca, and they are mentioned in the Qur'ān (53:19–22). In South Arabia they are called the "Daughters of Il," and al-Ilāt and al-'Uzzā are mentioned in Sabaean inscriptions.[17]

The Persian religion of Zoroastrianism, the state religion of the pre-Islamic Iranian empire, was also present in the region, which rested on the teachings of the mysterious Zoroaster, who taught dualistic ideas not dissimilar to the Greeks, in which an ultimate being (or unifying principle) was also posited. Zoroastrianism thus had both dualistic and monotheistic elements, and its call to honour a supreme deity is remarkably similar to that of Islam, as well as its emphasis on good works, heaven and hell. Zoroaster proclaimed that there is only one 'God,' the singularly creative and *sustaining force* of the Universe.[18]

We must not overlook that Christianity in Nestorian form had also made some inroads in the region and Arian as well as gnostic-type

---

Wadd ("Love") originated from North Arabia and probably was a moon god: the magic formula *Wd'b*, "Wadd is [my?] father," written on amulets and buildings, is often accompanied by a crescent Moon with the small disk of Venus. In Ḥaḍramawt the national god Syn was also a sun god: the current identification with the Mesopotamian moon god Sin (Suen) raises phonetic objections, and the symbolic animal of Syn, shown on coins, was the eagle, a solar animal. In Qatabān the national god 'Amm, "paternal uncle," may have been a moon god."

[17] Ryckmans, "Arabian Religion."

[18] See Mary Boyce, *Zoroastrians: Their Religious Beliefs and Practices* (London: Routledge & Kegan Paul, 1979).

sects were likely present in the region as well. [19] Moreover, John of Damascus, one of the great theologians in Christian intellectual history, who in the early part of the eighth century lived in the time of rapid Islamic expansion, considered Islam to be last in a line of pseudo-Christian heresies. Griffith tells us of John of Damascus, "he speaks of Muhammed as having been one who, 'having happened upon the Old and New Testaments, likewise having probably been in conversation with an Arian monk, contrived his own heresy.'"[20] Arianism was an early Unitarian cult according to which Jesus Christ was merely a creature and servant of God, not the eternal Son of God. It seems highly likely that these varied religious forces had a powerful influence on the Islamic formulation of the doctrine of Allah.

In the pagan thought of the region, then, since any supreme being is unknown and fundamentally mysterious, the world is ultimately governed by *fate*. Man is helpless before *Fortuna*,[21] and must seek some kind of protection or control via rituals, fetishes and sacrifices to influence the powers and appease the gods.[22] Considering the pagan religious milieu at the time of Islam's emergence (including the paganized versions of Christianity), the pre-Islamic worship of a supreme deity called Allah in the region, the ongoing significance of the Kaaba in Islam and the obligatory pilgrimage to Mecca, it is clear that the Allah to whom Muhammad was calling the Arabian world to return as the supreme deity, was not the Elohim of the covenant— it was not the God and Father of our Lord Jesus Christ. This is evident from the fact that Muhammad saw himself as re-*establishing* a faith that is quite contrary to Scripture.

This becomes especially clear when we consider the important Islamic doctrine of *Tawhid*. Remember, our primary concern at pres-

---

[19] Sidney H. Griffith, *The Church in the Shadow of the Mosque: Christians and Muslims in the World of Islam* (Princeton: Princeton University Press, 2008), 8.

[20] Griffith, *The Church in the Shadow*, 42.

[21] *Fortuna* is the Greco-Roman goddess of fortune or fate.

[22] For an excellent discussion of pre-Islamic deities and the religious influences on Islam see Ryckmans, "Arabian Religion," https://www.britannica.com/topic/Arabian-religion. The author writes: "The study of these practices is instructive in view of their similarities with those of the biblical world and also with those of the world of Islām, for, while firmly repudiating the idolatry of the pre-Islāmic period, which it calls the "Age of Ignorance" (Jāhilīyah), Islām has nevertheless taken over, in a refined form, some of its practices."

ent is with the *doctrine of God* as it emerges in Islamic thought and is propagated today. As we look at Islamic teaching concerning the divine it seems clear that the doctrine of Allah was deeply influenced by the dominant pagan concepts of *fate and the existence of a supreme primitive force* (an unknown god) that surrounded Islam's originators. In some respects, Islam appears to be an attempt to *synthesize* a pagan doctrine of god as an unknown and supreme *principle of fate* (essentially a nature religion) with a more Hebraic, Christian idea of *revelation* from a God who speaks into history. However, as we will see, this is an impossible dialectic so that in the process of attempting a synthesis, the biblical idea of God and revelation is radically perverted. In this way Islam gives us both a pagan nature religion *and* pseudo-Christian cultural religion as two poles of the same belief system. These are manifest in the fatalism, spiritualism, fetishism and mysticism inherent in the worship of the Islamic 'nature deity' that is quasi-pantheistic on the one hand, and the law, structure and political totalitarianism that manifests the cultural religion of 'revelation' on the other.

THE ISLAMIC DOCTRINE OF GOD
Central to the concept of *Allah* in Islam, then, is the doctrine of *Tawhid*—meaning *absolute oneness*, or unity. Although the word *Tawhid* does not appear in the Qur'an, the root word *wahad* appears many times. Its main aim is to deny any form of likeness or association whatsoever to god. It is difficult to overstate the importance of this concept in Islam: "Proclaim, He is Allah, the single" (Surah 112:1). That is, Allah is considered the One, the Only, the eternal, the absolute. As James White has pointed out, "Ask any sincere follower what defines Islam, and they will answer quickly. Tawhid, the glorious monotheistic truth, the heart of Islamic faith, is to the Muslim what the Trinity is to the Christian: the touchstone, the non-negotiable, the definitional."[23] On this view, Allah is completely and radically *incomparable* (Tanzih) to anything or anyone. Allah is distinct from *all associations* so that to attempt to know his nature is 'shirk,' the error of idolatry or polytheism. As Muhammed Abdul Rauf states,

---

[23] James R. White, *What Every Christian Needs to Know about the Qur'an* (Minneapolis, MN: Bethany, 2013), 59.

"God is the essence of existence. His Arabic name is Allah. He is The First and The Last. He is unique and nothing resembles Him in any respect. He is One and The One."[24] It is immediately striking that these descriptions are impersonal, monistic and ineffable.

The result of this formulation in Islamic thought is that to say anything truly theological about Allah becomes a form of idolatry—although ironically to speak of God as the 'essence of existence' and the 'First and Last' is to say something theological about Allah. Critically (and taking us back to our earlier point about the antithesis), both the Qur'an and Hadith attack the doctrine of the triune God of biblical Christianity as polytheism and a violation of the philosophical abstraction of *Tawhid* (Surah 2:116; 4:155,157–158,171; 5:17, 72,73; 19:92; 23:91; 39:4); though the Qur'an shows no evidence of coming close to an accurate understanding of the Christian formulation of the Trinity (Surah 5:116).[25] This serious failure of understanding is problematic for Islam because *first*, the Qur'an is meant to be absolutely without error as an eternal book that came down from heaven, and *second*, because it is clear that the Qur'anic author of these attacks on the Trinity clearly thought he *was* condemning the Christian formulation of the doctrine of God. Since it is plain that a considerable part of the purpose of the Qur'an is to refute scriptural teaching about God, it is highly problematic that it spends so much time refuting assertions not actually being made in biblical revelation and Christian theology.[26]

Nonetheless, what is important here is that these Qur'anic texts are a specific polemic against the Christian doctrine of God, insisting on the absolute *oneness* of Allah as a unitary being—a monad or singularity. Obviously, as soon as you say *anything* about such a being it ceases to be an incomparable unity—hence the Islamic resistance to 'theology.' The philosophical abstraction of *Tawhid* is not unlike the Greek conclusion of an ultimate and absolute unity or oneness at the root of all being (found in the thought of Plotinus), or the

[24] Muhammad Abdul Rauf, *Islam Creed and Worship* (Washington, DC: The Islamic Centre, 1974), 2–3.
[25] One Islamic school of thought holds that the Trinity is composed of essentially three gods, Allah, Maryam and Isa, suggesting a kind of union between Maryam and Allah.
[26] See White, *What Every Christian Needs to Know*, 86, 98.

ultimacy of being, or even non-being, found in Buddhism. Of this absolute One, nothing can really be said or ascribed, for then it would cease to be an *absolute unity*. Consequently, you cannot do a 'theology' of the One God in Islam, because its nature is wholly unknown. As the former Islamic jurist and now Christian scholar of Islam, Sam Solomon, has pointed out:

> 'Theology' is not applicable within Islamic scholarship, but would be considered a term of great offence. Thus, for a Muslim, for one to infer that mankind could apprehend or understand anything about Allah's actual nature, or to even venture to question what the Qur'an says about Allah is a legally punishable offense.[27]

It is therefore something of a profound irony to discover that Allah is given ninety-nine names in Islam! The Muslim seeks to escape this logical conundrum by asserting that none of these names actually refer to God's *nature*, thereby hoping to preserve *Tawhid*.

It thus follows from the doctrine of *Tawhid*, and the remote unknowability of the divine, that Allah never speaks directly to people but only through intermediaries—recall the ancient Greek notion of demons who bring messages from god. As one leading Islamic scholar argues:

> If someone asks Allah to pronounce His Unity (Oneness) Himself directly without any channel, He would rejoin: This is below My dignity to address my creatures directly. Nor any human is permitted to talk to me without any 'medium.' Allah has revealed in the Holy Qur'an "And no one can dare speak to Allah." (Surah 42:51).[28]

The Allah of Islam is therefore a non-relational god, who will forever be unknowable and unknown. The spiritual intermediaries

---

[27] Sam Solomon with Atif Debs, *Not the Same God: Is the Qur'anic Allah the Lord God of the Bible?* (Charlottesville, VA: ANM Publishers, 2015), 16.

[28] Dr. Muhammad Tahir-ul-Qadri, *Spiritualism and Magnetism* (Lahore: Minhaj-ul-Qur'an Publications, 2001), 100.

don't *know* Allah any more than anyone else. This is the logical out-working of a strictly monadic conception of God as absolute unity (monism). Such a 'god' is reduced to an abstract philosophical principle that cannot be personal, relational or have any meaningful contact with creation. Any doctrine related to Allah in Islam therefore can only be stated in terms of negation—who Allah is not—since he is ultra-transcendent and relationless. Relationality is in no sense essential to his being, "Allah does not speak to any one directly… nobody can establish any direct communication with Allah."[29]

Since this unknowable god can neither be comprehended nor truly reveal himself (more properly 'itself'), three things result. *First*, the only conceivable 'contact' with (i.e. experience of) such an impersonal *principle of being* is through the spiritualist, non-rational encounter of the mystic. It is therefore no surprise to find that, by tradition, Muhammad spent weeks in a cave on Mount Hira in the 'remembrance of Allah' and, in the process allegedly envisioned true dreams.[30] Here he claimed private supernatural encounters. From the Islamic sources we learn that he was troubled by these mystical experiences and was worried about being possessed by a Jinn (spirit). He even contemplated suicide because of the deeply troubling nature of the visions and incidents.[31] This is an aspect of Islam as *nature* or *mystery religion* that seeks mystical encounter with an *unknown being*. In the tradition of the revered Imam al-Ghazali, Tahir-ul Qadri writes, "Mysticism is the only means of the internal experiences and observations…. Mysticism brings about the internal observation of the faith to the zenith of certainty."[32]

Second, given the doctrine of *Tawhid*, the unknown unity or principle of being that is Allah steadily becomes indistinguishable from 'nature' and 'fate' itself, because *everything* becomes an expression of the will of 'god.' And *third*, since this 'god' cannot speak to man, an intermediary is required to 'stand in' for Allah to reveal and embody the will of this unknowable absolute One—the one will in the universe. How an absolute unity can have any 'will'—since the concept of

29 Tahir-ul-Qadri, *Spiritualism and Magnetism*, 101.
30 Tahir-ul-Qadri, *Spiritualism and Magnetism*, 27.
31 See White, *What Every Christian Needs to Know*, 22–25.
32 Tahir-ul-Qadri, *Spiritualism and Magnetism*, 24.

will involves the ideas of distinction, personhood and relationship—is unexplained and cannot be questioned in Islam. The *Shahadah*, the Islamic creed, states: "No deity but Allah and Muhammad is the Messenger of Allah." In this fashion Muhammad establishes himself as the sole intermediary and arbiter of true religion, and his *Sunnah* (example in sayings and deeds) become the pattern of true religion for all time.

THE NATURE MOTIVE IN ISLAM

Understanding the doctrine of Allah as grounded in *Tawhid* enables us to grasp the origin of the first aspect of the religious core of Islam—*nature or fate*. Although Allah is meant to be *transcendent*, his absolute unity inevitably leads to a philosophical form of pantheism or *total immanence* which produces voluntarism[33] and fatalism. MacDonald observes that "it is part of the irony of the history of Muslim theology that the very emphasis on the transcendental unity should lead thus to pantheism."[34] Pantheism is the very essence of *nature religion*. Ineluctably on this conception of Allah, everything is gradually incorporated into the One.

The famed Muslim thinker Al-Ghazali was Persian and deeply influenced by the Sufi tradition in Islam, as well as Neo-Platonism via certain forms of Christian theology.[35] He reported from his mystic encounters that, "Indeed there is nothing in existence except God and His acts, for whatever is there besides Him is His act." In another work he argues that mystics "are able to see visually that there is no being in the world other than God and that the face of everything is perishable save His face (Surah 28:88)...indeed, everything other than He, considered in itself, is pure nonbeing...therefore, nothing is except God Almighty and His face."[36] Although one of Allah's names, *Al Haqq*, means pure transcendence, the concept of transcendence essentially denotes *distinction*. But since there is no distinction basic to Allah's own being (as a pure monadic unity), he cannot be

---

[33] Voluntarism is the idea that *will* is the fundamental or dominant factor in the universe.

[34] G. B. MacDonald, cited in Reilly, *The Closing*, 111.

[35] See John M. Frame, *A History of Western Philosophy and Theology* (Phillipsburg, NJ: P&R Publishing, 2015), 141.

[36] Al-Ghazali, cited in Reilly, *The Closing*, 110.

truly transcendent by nature. At best, Allah's 'transcendence' can only be *co-relative* to the world, which means 'god' is interdependent on the world and an evolving being, defined by nature—the essence of paganism.

Inevitably, this type of distinction (co-relativity between God and the world) proves to be less than fully real. Whether the Muslim realizes it or not, Allah is really the god of pagan pantheism, akin to Indian philosophy in which the world as created being is an illusion (Maya). In Islam, philosophically, reality is merely semblance because Allah is the One and Only. This leads to the progressive denial of real natural (or creational) phenomena, so that genuine cause-and-effect relations steadily break down. It is true that formally the Muslim wants to reject pantheism; in fact, Sunni Islam rejected Islamic philosophy in part because it embraced Aristotle's emanationism (creation as emanation from God). Yet at the same time it incorporated Sufism—the most philosophically consistent brand of Islam—through al-Ghazali's teaching. Sufism is basically Gnosticism rooted in the mystic leap toward the unknowable absolute.

The problem for Islam is that without an essential distinction of persons within God's own being (where God is both ultimate subject and object) so that, by subject-object relation, differentiation, predication, thought, knowledge, will, purpose, act and love (morality) can find a starting point in the infinite personal, there is no basis for the idea of creation as a free and intelligible act. Absent the triune God of the Bible, Islam provides no basis for reason, historical revelation or a supra-rational knowledge of God. As a result, the *transcendence* of Allah's absolute unity collapses into *pure immanence*—Allah is all and is identified with all events so that life is sheer fate. Thus Ibn Arabi concluded from his reading of the primary sources that "Allah is all and all is Allah" as set out in his treatise, *Al-Futuhat al Makkiya*, which is studied today by Muslim scholars and remains in great demand throughout the Islamic world.[37] It is vitally important to see, then, that Islam proves *unable to make a meaningful or coherent distinction between Allah and nature*—they collapse into one. As Ibn Arabi stated, "in the last analysis, Allah himself is the spirit of the

---

37 See Solomon, *Not the Same God*, 108.

cosmos, while the cosmos is his body."[38] This is far from the scriptural concept of creation, but as Solomon observes regarding Allah, "Although he is called 'the creator' his creation was brought into being remotely, without his personal involvement with his creation."[39] To be self-aware, one must have something distinct from oneself to reflect upon, and since Allah is a pure and *simple unity*, before creation he is not self-aware and so the cosmos is reduced to involuntary *emanation*, not a free act of creation.

The *nature motive* in Islamic religion, springing from this pagan concept of god, means that the distinction between Allah and nature—including man—is essentially obliterated. As a consequence we find situations like Abu Yazid al Bistami (d. 875) speaking of his mystical encounter with the absolute, claiming self-extinction in ecstatic encounter, and a self-identification with the divine, "Glory be to me, how great is my worth...within this robe is naught but Allah."[40] Given the nature of Allah, Al-Ghazali came to the logical conclusion that the only true contact with divinity comes from mystic encounter with the absolute. He said, "by means of this con-templation of heavenly forms and images they rise by degrees to heights which human language cannot reach."[41] The echoes of Plato's thought forms here are striking.

Because of Islam's unknowable god who becomes indistinguishable from nature itself, the idea of a rational universe of cause and effect relations gradually retreats from view. A real secondary causality becomes incoherent and *everything* becomes an aspect of Allah's will. An Imam in Pakistan recently instructed physicists there that they should not consider the idea of cause and effect in their work:

> Dr. Pervez Hoodbhoy, a Pakistani physicist and professor at Quaid-e-Azam University in Islamabad said that, "it was not Islamic to say that combining hydrogen and oxygen makes water." You were supposed to say that when you bring hydrogen and oxygen together then by the will of Allah water was created.[42]

---

[38] Solomon, *Not the Same God*, 108 n56.

[39] Solomon, *Not the Same God*, 136, 139, 170.

[40] Cited in Reilly, *The Closing*, 106.

[41] Cited in Reilly, *The Closing*, 108.

[42] Cited in Reilly, *The Closing*, 142.

Nature and Allah are so closely identified that everything which occurs in the material world is simply an expression of Allah's direct will—indeed Allah is impersonal, *pure will* or *pure force* (though we have seen that, given the doctrine of *Tawhid*, a personal will of God cannot be theoretically accounted for). In such a view human will has no derived independent existence. Inevitably, the good and evil deeds of man become equally ultimate, both resulting from the direct and immediate will of Allah.

The end product of this *nature motive* is an entrenched *fatalistic apathy* in Islamic culture which is clearly expressed in the deeply religious phrase *inshallah* (if it be Allah's will). As Reilly has commented, "If man lives in a world of which he can make no sense, an irrational world without causality, he can choose only to surrender to fate or to despair. Reason and freedom become irrelevant."[43] In Islam then, *nature* is actually a conflation of 'god' and the 'world' as co-relative (a cosmos reduced to semblance), with Allah as an absolute and unknowable Oneness. Philosophically this god is ultimately indistinguishable from apparent phenomena and historical eventuation.

THE CULTURAL MOTIVE OF ISLAM

I have argued that in Islam a blank and non-relational divinity concept stands behind the twin poles of a *nature/fate religious aspect* (inshallah) on the one hand and a *cultural religious aspect* of social order on the other—a culture based in a *revelation of law* and social custom through Muhammad. Since a *nature religion* grounded in fate or pure will cannot produce a transcendent and objective standard for social order or moral truth, the opposite pole in Islam's ground motive is *revelation*, in which the paradise idea is foremost and *culture*, in the form of a human archetype, is absolutized. The *ummah* (world community of Islam) becomes the material goal of Islam in order to introduce some kind of coherence into its fatalistic cosmos governed by an unknown god. In other words, since the being called Allah is unknown and unknowable and effectively *co-relative* to the world, a god whose will is indistinguishable from what occurs in nature, an objective and identifiable standard becomes necessary to

---

43 Reilly, *The Closing*, 129.

concretize the Islamic faith—*a cultural motive grounded in an idea of revelation.*

However, the *cultural aspect of historical revelation* in Islam is in clear and irresolvable dialectical tension with the other pole—the *nature aspect.* This is because, *first,* a doctrine of revelation requires a real transcendence (distinction) of God over creation. Only a being truly distinct from and transcending time and history can speak into a creation history that is truly other, i.e. a history that is not merely an aspect of divine emanation. *Second,* as we have seen, Islam teaches that Allah is an absolute and non-relational unity, both unknown and unknowable, so the concept of revelation (a personal and relational act) is incoherent in Islam. *Third,* how can a special revelation *even be identified* if *everything* that occurs is in fact a revelation of Allah's *direct* and immediate will?

In an effort to overcome these problems, it is claimed that the Qur'an is itself a copy of an *eternal book* in Arabic (co-relative to Allah), that is revelatory of *Allah's will.*[44] However, this introduces a whole new set of apparently irresolvable problems in connecting Islam's *nature divinity* with a cultural religion of *revelation.* For example, since monistic concepts of god logically lead to mystical self-realization (which did develop in Sufism as we have noted), and not the biblical idea of historical revelation from a personal God who speaks and *reveals himself,* how is the idea of revelation coherent in Islam? How can Allah be the One and Only incomparable absolute unity if there is in fact a co-eternal text in Arabic next to him in paradise that lays out his will? Surely, on Islam's own terms, the notion of an *eternal* book is *shirk* (idolatry) and setting up something next to God? Moreover, how can a temporally-revealed book, addressing the immediate circumstances arising in the historical life of Muhammad, be an eternal entity, next to an unknowable and non-relational Allah—a 'being' logically unconcerned with creation and utterly remote from history? Perhaps even more problematic for this dialectic is how an incomparable, non-relational, unknowable being, in a world where God has no image-bearer, could give 'revelation' that is recognizable and comprehensible to man. To these questions Islam offers no coherent answer. It is blasphemous for the

---

[44] White, *What Every Christian Needs to Know,* 19.

Muslim to even ask them. The Islamic response is to reassert the *Shahadah*, "there is no god but God [*Tawhid*] and Muhammad is the messenger of God."

Absolutely fundamental to Islam, then, is the remarkable status accorded to the *man* Muhammad, for without Muhammad there can be no Islam. At the root of the *cultural motive* in Islam (grounded in the concept of revelation) is this allegedly peerless personage. We have made the crucial observation that between the Islamic divinity concept (Allah) and the man Muhammad is postulated an *eternal form* (another debt to Greek philosophy), co-extensive with God, called the Qur'an. However, the temporal cultural embodiment of that eternal form is actually found in *Muhammad himself* who, being the receptacle and vehicle of that revelation (mediated via *jinn*), constitutes the *archetype* for the *cultural religion* of Islam—which is the only distinctive idea that Islam introduces. But given the non-relational and unknowable nature of Allah, what can carry the 'revelation' from such an abstract oneness (being) to the man Muhammad? In Islamic literature and tradition it is the angel Gabriel—which is clearly an idea borrowed from the Bible, being as incongruent with the Islamic idea of God as the idea of revelation itself. The sudden appearance of Father Christmas in *The Chronicles of Narnia* seems more plausible in context than the appearance of Gabriel in the Islamic account of Muhammad's revelations, given the nature of Allah and Islamic worldview.

It is equally important to note at this point that despite Muhammad's status and revelations, he himself cannot do anything to save the individual—he cannot deliver anyone from the unfathomable swerve and deadly jaws of fate (Allah's will). However, he sets forth the *eternal will* in a series of *revelations* thought to be *a copy of an eternal form*, which in a certain sense, since Allah is reduced to pure will, is identical with Allah. As a result, the will of Allah and the teaching and life-model of Muhammad are so closely identified as to practically (while not doctrinally) absolutize Muhammad. To illustrate, consider some of the names ascribed to Muhammad: The Highest; Most Beautiful; The Truth itself; The Mighty One; The Sign of Allah; The Light; Allah's Grace; Language itself; The Sanctifier;

The Grantor of Pardon; The Diadem—to name but a few![45] If these are not descriptions of a man turned demi-god, it is difficult to know what would be sufficient to essentially divinize an individual. This is why the older term 'Muhammadan' is the most technically appropriate term for the Muslim, because it is really only Muhammad that is allegedly 'known' in Islam and whose example must be followed. As Solomon points out:

> After labouring over the need NOT to humanize Allah or to divinize a man, the Qur'an singles out Mohammed, a mere man, to be the embodiment of the mercies of Allah.... Hence there is nothing and no part of Islam that can be understood or handled without Muhammed, be it Islamic beliefs, Islamic practices, Islamic doctrines, Islamic Shari'ah, Islamic conduct, Islamic dress codes, Islamic diet—and much more...based on what every ancient and modern Muslim scholar without exception has said and written, Allah and his "messenger" Muhammed, are inseparable, and no distinction can be made between them.[46]

In this way the *cultural aspect* of life in Islam is *absolutized* and the model and teaching of a mortal and sinful man is made an eternal and irrevocable standard. Muhammad becomes the only concrete link between the divine being and man and obedience to Muhammad is equated with obedience to God himself (see Surah 3:31–32,132; 4:13–14,59,69,80; 5:92; 9:71).

We have already noted that Sufi mysticism is the natural outgrowth of the *nature motive* in Islam. True experience of divine being is only by mystical encounter. The Sufi practice (while not denying the importance of Muhammad) emphasizes the *nature deity*, not the *cultural motive* in Islam, making Sufis typically more tolerant and peaceable in practice than some other sects. However, when the cultural motive is accentuated, Islam centres on the life of Muhammad, not mysticism, thus emphasizing his social and cultural example. This revelatory example is said to be the final *absolute rule of life as*

---

45 The list of honorifics goes on. See Solomon, *Not the Same God*, 123–134.
46 Solomon, *Not the Same God*, 138, 146–147.

modelled by the last true prophet. Since Islam claims kinship with biblical faith (claiming everyone from Adam, to Abraham and Jesus for itself) all previous revelations must be understood in terms of Muhammad and any contradictions to his claims and teachings in Hebrew and Christian revelation *must* be due to their deliberate corruption.

Muhammad therefore represents the cultural embodiment of an eternal form. Allah is absolute being, pure form, pure will and, *limited by such a boundary,* cannot pass from the realm of abstraction and non-relational Oneness to the realm of history. However, Muhammad, via private Qur'anic revelations, incarnates God's pure will and thereby historically *takes the place of the divine.* As such, the *cultural aspect* of life is absolutized and the *ummah* is essentially *divinized* by imitating Muhammad's example. This means that nothing is more important than the Muslim community and the cultural advance of Islam as the very embodiment of god's will.

This cultural project is driven by an underlying *paradise motive.* Muhammad is again the key to paradise and the attainment of a kind of Elysium.[47] As the heroic cultural warrior and embodiment of divine will, Muhammad promises victory for Islam and a coming world governed by Islam. Those that strive in his cause therefore have the best chance of paradise. Bynum has written of this phenomenon,

> It is the *deification of a cultural system.* . . . in this view, the cultural structure essentially replaces the concept of a living God and thus human freedom, happiness and ultimately lives are sacrificed to the cultural form in proportion to the fanaticism engendered by the belief in it.[48]

Thus, where the *cultural motive* of Islam is stressed above the *nature motive*, instead of producing the primacy of mystical encounter with the divine as in Sufism, Islam is pursued as the final and only authen-

---

[47] Elysium is a conception of paradise maintained by some Greek religious and philosophical sects. Admission was initially reserved for mortals related to the gods and other heroes. Later, it expanded to include those chosen by the gods, the righteous, and the heroic, where they would remain after death, to live a blessed and happy life, and *indulging in whatever employment they had enjoyed in life.*

[48] Bynum, *Allah,* 21.

tic religion that will conquer the world politically and culturally by bringing everything else into forceful subjugation to Muhammad and his successors. Allah is one and is all and Muhammad is his prophet, so Islam must crush all opposition. The inherent threat is that the sole vindication of Muhammad's claims must be the *cultural victory* of Islam via the imposition of *Shari'ah* (Allah's will) on all the world and the subjugation or conversion of the infidel (non-Muslim). This drive was basic to Islam from its inception. In an early text written in Greek (c. 634), the author tells of the incursion of the Arabs and a false prophet who appeared among them. Griffith writes:

> The text reports a question put to a learned Jew, "What can you tell me about the prophet who has appeared with the Saracens?" To which he replied, "He is false, for the prophets do not come armed with a sword," and the learned man avers that the prophet may in fact be the Antichrist. Then, according to the text, the questioner made further inquiries and he "heard from those who had met him that there was no truth to be found in the so-called prophet, only the shedding of men's blood. He says also that he has the keys of paradise, which is incredible."[49]

These Christian repudiations of Islam reappear constantly in later Christian texts which summarize the new religion of Islam as defined by bloodshed, the spirit of Antichrist and the hope of a carnal, sensual paradise. However, despite the objections of Jews, Christians and those of other faiths, the *form* of Allah's will, manifest in Muhammad's life and example, must be replicated everywhere as an expression of the eternal will. As such, Islam can only be incarnated (rather than solely mystical in private experience) in terms of the concreteness of a *cultural religion of revelation* that of necessity absolutizes a human being by transforming him into something like an Olympian god. As Bynum has observed:

> Islam crystalizes the worship of man both in the concept of the ummah, or "community of believers" which takes absolute precedence over the individual, and also in the worshipful

---

49 Griffith, *The Church in the Shadow of the Mosque*, 24–25.

veneration of one specific man, Muhammed, so much so that the tiniest details of his personal habits are imitated to this day. His likes and dislikes along with the sayings and doings of Muhammed form the entire basis for good and evil in the Islamic system. There is no other measure. In Islam, man (in abstract) is not the measure of all things; one specific man is. Islam puts man in place of God.[50]

Islam's self-vindication, indeed the only possible justification of Islam's truthfulness, is not by reasoned argument—for Allah is neither reason nor reasonable. Nor is the validation of Islam by the grace of God and working of God's Spirit of truth—for Allah is neither grace nor truth. Allah is *pure force*, pure will, so *the only vindication of pure force, is force.* As Reilly points out, "The rule of power is the natural, logical outcome of a voluntaristic theology that invests God's shadow on earth—the caliph or ruler—with an analogous force based on God's will."[51] It is for this reason that the striving world of Islam is perpetually at war, if not militarily, then culturally, with the *kafir*—an insulting term for the non-believer who conceals the truth of Islam. Pure will or force manifest for all time in the life and teaching of Muhammad does not reason or debate but imposes (see Surah 2:216; 4:89; 9:29; 47:4; 61:10). This is why Islam, from the time and historic example of Muhammad, spread through the sword:

> In Mecca, Mohammed was a religious preacher who converted about 10 people a year to Islam. In Medina, Mohammed was a warrior and politician who converted about 10,000 people to Islam every year. Politics and Jihad were a thousand times more effective than religion to convert the Arabs to Islam.[52]

In the process of this conquest, Islam stamps out plurality, freedom and liberty for a strictly unitary and totalitarian understanding of

---

[50] Bynum, *Allah*, 34.

[51] Reilly, *The Closing*, 131.

[52] Bill Warner, *Sharia Law for Non-Muslims* (Nashville, TN: Center for the Study of Political Islam, 2010), 23.

social, cultural and political life as an inevitable reflection of its conception of the divine.

Once Islamic culture ceased to be able to conquer and thereby parasitically live off the cultural energy of largely Christian peoples,[53] the Islamic world was left to its own resources and steadily stagnated—which is where almost all the Islamic nations are today. Those that have prospered to a degree have only done so either because of former colonial influence on their institutions or the development of their natural resources through a massive Western investment of technology and the purchase of oil.

THE CHRISTIAN WITNESS

Though superficially dressed in the garb of Abrahamic faith, we have seen that Islam, with its defective monistic concept of god emerging from pagan roots, collapses the divine, and with it all the cosmos, into the One, the Only—an unknown and unknowable essence of pure will that logically identifies god with fate (*inshallah*). I have called this the *nature motive* within Islam because absolute being is effectively truncated to *pure force* and creation is essentially reduced to emanation (the body of god) from an absolute, ineffable Oneness. By stressing the Oneness and arbitrary will of the divine being, the value of what happens in the world is diminished, free human action is denied and the thought of escaping into a carnal paradise becomes paramount for the Muslim.

Since such a view of the divine is basically non-rational, fatalistic and anti-cultural, in order for Islam to be a social force, it was necessary for an opposite pole to be held in tension with *nature* (Allah). I have called this opposite pole the *cultural motive*—a principle of law based in the idea of *revelation* of which Muhammad is the archetype and effective mediator, making Muhammadanism a cultural religion that absolutizes a man and his community—the

---

[53] The philosophical and translation movements of the classical Islamic cultural period are the most noteworthy example of the borrowed learning of the Arab civilization that followed the allegedly illiterate Muhammad out of the desert to conquer the Arabian Peninsula and beyond. The early Caliphate, prior to the crusades, was packed with Christian physicians, logicians, philosophers, mathematicians, copyists and translators who were among the conquered Christian nations and peoples. See Griffith, *The Church in the Shadow of the Mosque*, 106–128.

cultural aspect of human experience. Islam thereby "saves society from the anarchy inherent in its philosophy by imposing ultra-strict totalitarian social regulation."[54] Consequently a veil comes down over freedom, individuality, plurality and beauty—as typified when a woman's face is covered or music is banished. The imposition of *Shari'ah* to govern all aspects of life thus asserts a radical and absolute unity at the expense of diversity.

Biblical revelation, by contrast, reveals the *triune God* as the key to all human thought, all creation, all truth and all reality. This God is a personal, relational and covenant-making God who speaks to his creatures and enters into relationship with them as a Father. In his high priestly prayer, Jesus made plain that God had manifested himself so that people might enter the intimacy of fellowship with the triune God and know him in familial terms. In radical contrast to Islam, God is to be known intimately: "And this is eternal life, that they *know you*, the only true God, and Jesus Christ whom you have sent" (John 17:3 ESV) And since, according to Scripture, man is made in the *image of God*, it tells us of the incarnation of God the eternal Son as man, the exact imprint of God's own nature and thus fully representational of God. Immediately we have in Christ something comparable to the invisible and immortal God—the incarnate Word, Jesus Christ—because he is fully God and fully man. Moreover, man is God's image-bearer, which tells us something about who God is. Perhaps most remarkable of all, through Christ, God sends his Holy Spirit to dwell in us so that we have immediate fellowship with God without a need for angels and mediums to mediate for us.

Jesus Christ reveals a God who is himself an eternal community of love (John 17:5), both *one and many*, unity in diversity, so that transcendence (distinction) is essential to his own being. The Scriptures further reveal that of his own *free will* he called all creation into being (so he is not co-relative to the world), and as both sovereign Lord and creator he both transcends creation as an absolute personality, while being immanent within it, upholding all things by his powerful law-Word. The distinction within God's own being, which implies God's distinction from the world, means that he transcends creation, while still able to be immanent within it, animating it by

---

54 Bynum, *Allah*, 150.

his Spirit, without contradiction. Critically, this distinction—an inter-subjectivity that exists between the persons of the Godhead—is the basis upon which knowledge, love, freedom, will and purpose are grounded and find their starting point. The God and Father of our Lord Jesus Christ is able to communicate and reveal himself, and access to the divine is not limited to a few mystics, but made available to *all* through the death and resurrection of Christ.

Likewise, *revelation* in the Christian gospel is not an eternal book (eternal form) taken from a shelf of abstraction co-relative to God, but is rather ultimately manifest in the *person* of Jesus Christ in history. The God of Scripture speaks, and that revelation is finally of himself in his Son, communicated by the work of the Holy Spirit. God has chosen to reveal himself to us also in the infallible written Word of God, which is the account and testimony of that revelation of the Son and his redemptive work. Since God's covenant Word is revealed in time and history to God's servants, it was inscripturated for our life and instruction. This written Word, which points us to Christ, is taken by God the Holy Spirit and quickened to human minds and hearts for our regeneration and transformation. It speaks to and constitutes human understanding, but it does so in a manner that frees the God-given potential inherent in created rationality. As Colin Gunton has put it:

> The Word is the focus of rationality, enabling us to conceive the relatedness of man and nature; while within that structure the Spirit is the focus of freedom.... What becomes conceivable as a result of such a development is an understanding of particularity which guards against the pressure to homogeneity.... Both cosmologically and socially, we may say, there is need to give priority neither to the one nor to the many. Being is diversity within unity.[55]

This understanding of who God is, as revealed in the gospel, gives rise to a social and cultural vision that values unity within diversity,

---

[55] Colin E. Gunton, *The One the Three and the Many: God, Creation and the Culture of Modernity*, The 1992 Brampton Lectures (Cambridge: Cambridge University Press, 1993), 212.

plurality and freedom under God's order, while resisting tyranny and the totalitarian impulse. This gospel unveils relational love to God and neighbour as the centre of human well-being and it offers the gospel of the kingdom freely and without compulsion. In a manner inconceivable within Islam, the gospel of Jesus Christ provides relationality and sociality because of who God is, and because of his redemptive purposes within creation. Gunton's conclusion is brilliant:

> Personal beings are social beings, so that of both God and man it must be said they have their being in their personal related-ness: their free relation-in-otherness. This is not so of the rest of creation, which does not have the marks of love and freedom which are among the marks of the personal. Of the universe as a whole we should conclude that it is marked by relationality rather than sociality. All things are what they are by being par-ticulars constituted by many and various forms of relation.[56]

He goes on to show that this biblical reality has an important cultural implication:

> Relationality is thus the transcendental which allows us to learn something of what it is to say that all created people and things are marked by their coming from and returning to the God who is himself in his essential and inmost being, a being in rela-tion.... Redemption thus means the redirection of the partic-ular to its own end and not a re-creation. *The distinctive feature of created persons is their mediating function in the achievement of perfection by the rest of creation. They are called to the forms of action, in science, ethics and art—in a word, to culture—which enable to take place the sacrifice of praise, which is the free offering of all things, perfected, to their creator.* Theologically put, the created world becomes truly itself—moves toward its comple-tion—when through Christ and the Spirit, it is presented perfect before the throne of the Father. The sacrifice of praise which is the due human response to both creation and redemption

---

[56] Gunton, *The One*, 229.

takes the form of that culture which enables both personal and non-personal worlds to realise their true being.[57]

Islam is not a sacrifice of praise enabling a person to realize their true being in God's kingdom, offering all things perfected to their creator. Rather it is slavery to a philosophical and cultural idol. The Muslim hopes to escape the arbitrary fate of the unknown, unknowable and non-communicative Allah by means of the *cultural religion* of Muhammad, whose life and example are the slavish link and only contact point with an abstract, illusory world. Islam thus proves to be a very poor copy of Christianity, with Islamic culture (*ummah*) a superficial parody of the kingdom of God. In the end that cultural order is focused on an *absolutized man* who, unable to save, only points the way to a possible escape from the miseries of fate into an egocentric, libidinous paradise.

Precious people who are Muslims are prisoners of a false and self-destructive system, set up against the knowledge of God that robs them of their true humanity and of knowing the Lord and Saviour Jesus Christ, whose love and mercy is extended to them in the gospel. This same Christ has promised that not only will the believer *see him*, but shall be *like him*, because we will see God the Son as he is, and thereby know the living God as he is (1 John 3:2); this alone meets the religious longing of the Muslim to know the divine and find a kingdom of joy that never ends. We must share the good news of the Lord Jesus Christ, and witness faithfully to the wonder of being enfolded in the loving embrace of the triune God, with our Muslim friends, family and neighbours. And we ourselves must be strengthened in the knowledge that Jesus promised, "Do not be afraid; I am the First and the Last. I am He who lives, and was dead, and behold, I am alive forevermore" (Revelation 1:17–18 NKJV).

---

57 Gunton, *The One*, 230–31.

6

COMPREHENSIVE GOSPEL WITNESS AND THE LIFE OF WILLIAM WILBERFORCE

FOR AS THE BODY APART FROM THE SPIRIT IS DEAD, SO ALSO
FAITH APART FROM WORKS IS DEAD (JAMES 2:26 ESV).

COMPREHENSIVE GOSPEL WITNESS AFFIRMS A COMPREHENSIVE CHRISTIANITY

Our brief study of the nature and task of gospel witness has high-lighted the centrality of the biblical view of the heart for human understanding; the important role of worldviews in shaping thinking and behaviour; the character and strategy of the apologist when witnessing to unbelievers; and the two dominant religious strong-holds resisting those serious about sharing the faith in the West today. However, a consideration of our Christian calling to bear witness to the truth of the kingdom of God would not be complete without reflection upon the *comprehensive nature* of our witness. The gospel is not merely information to be shared verbally, it is new life and living truth to be worked out and applied in every area of life, otherwise it is not the gospel of the kingdom revealed in Scripture.

We have seen that the gospel concerns the revelation of a person, Jesus Christ, who is the Truth—the living Word of God. The comprehensive character of our witness concerning his lordship over every area of life and thought is correlated to the comprehensive nature of God's law-Word for creation and the restoration of that creation-order in the gospel. We witness, not simply to a narrow core of biblical themes concerning forgiveness of sin and justification by faith, though these doctrines are critical and should not be neglected. We testify to the truth of the entirety of the biblical world- and life-view as it unfolds in the narrative of Scripture, centred in the king-ship of the man Jesus Christ. In the process, we defend a full-orbed scriptural philosophy of life.

We are bound to do this because of who Jesus Christ is. In the prologue of John's Gospel we learn that Christ is the eternal Word of God through whom all things were made. Christ is portrayed in Scripture as the mediator of creation because all things were made through him and for him (John 1:1–16; Hebrews 1:2). Moreover, he sustains all things by his powerful Word (Hebrews 1:2–3). According to Paul,

> everything was created by Him, in heaven and on earth, the visible and the invisible, whether thrones or dominions or rulers or authorities— all things have been created through Him and for Him. He is before all things, and by Him all things hold together (Colossians 1:16–17).

Though we live in a fallen world into which we preach this gospel of the kingdom, everything created was made good by Christ Jesus, the living and eternal Word—the visible and invisible, including thrones and dominions, rulers and authorities. This is why for Christ's sake we are to submit ourselves to the authorities and ordinances that God has instituted (Gk. *created*) among men (1 Peter 2:13). God's created order is a law-order. The totality of creation of which Christ is mediator is no chaos. Everything in all creation is *subject* to Christ's law-Word (laws and norms), whether the stars in their courses, marriage and family, the church and state, arts and culture. All things are to be governed and *normed* by Christ's *Word-revelation*—they are to conform to his command. This fact is integral to the gospel and therefore our witness to it. Scripture reveals that this Word-revelation is made known first in creation and is republished in the glorious gospel of our redemption by the *incarnate Word* and inscripturated to make us wise for salvation.

Because the gospel of the kingdom contains, in the message of redemption, a republication of God's law-Word for *all creation* mediated by Christ the king, the Great Commission at the end of Matthew's Gospel sends out God's people as witnesses in terms of Jesus' *total authority* in heaven and in earth, charging us to teach everything the living Word has commanded, making disciples of the nations (Matthew 28:18–20). Given the identity of Christ as the Word of God, his exalted place, supremacy and absolute authority as mediator of creation and redemption, this final charge to the disciples is clearly *comprehensive* in scope. Our witness to the truth involves much more than simply sharing our testimony of personal salvation and forgiveness of sins—it includes this, but surely encapsulates the *totality* of our renewed lives and Christ's redemptive purpose for the whole cosmos. Given this truth, our witness must be lived out through every aspect of our being, in the totality of our thinking and in every area of our lives. Our apologetic is not restricted to propositions and concepts. It must involve the practical application of the gospel for people to see the Lord reigns.

COMPREHENSIVE GOSPEL WITNESS DOES NOT FORGET THE FAITHFUL

These considerations force upon us the great question every Christian must grapple with in our time: *How will the powerful Word-revelation of God relate to our life and witness in the world?* Will we try and restrict that Word-revelation to an "upper storey" of reality dealing with "spiritual matters," where the gospel is presented as salvation for the "soul" and the Scriptures are seen as a word for one's personal life and the institutional church while family, society, vocation, public life and culture are permitted to go their own way? Or will we present and live out the gospel as a life, culture and creation-renewing power?[1] The answer that we arrive at will determine not only the path of our personal life but the course of our culture and the nation's future.

In order to come to the right answer and recover a comprehensive gospel we need godly examples and models to follow that can resource us in a time of apostasy from scriptural faith. This brings us to one of the most important founders of modern evangelicalism, the remarkable English reformer William Wilberforce. He was in no doubt about the nature of the critical relation between the gospel and our life in the world when he went into battle for the installation of the creational and redemptive Word-revelation of Christ in the socio-cultural and political life of Great Britain. His extraordinary career only magnifies a tragic reality facing us today: many such heroes of the faith are being routinely ignored by the church or their specific scriptural motivations and convictions are supressed or airbrushed out of the story. Klaas Schilder's diagnosis of this modern tendency in sobering:

> The old saying is promptly proven right that a dying people ignores its great men. A glorious heritage claims responsibility for the future: individuals and nations, which have stood in first ranks, should maintain their place. As long as a people maintains its greatness, it will *know its history and honour its great men*. But when there is apostasy, one will rather not hear the strict exhortations of the past. In such days, people will belittle the same miracles which once had made them proud. They will ridicule their history and despise their great men, so that the crooked and wayward children will not feel shame when the memory and image of the great and mighty fathers beckon them.[2]

Seeking escape from the shame of faithlessness, many professing Christians have foolishly joined in the West's present obsession with

---

[1] For a full consideration of the scope of the gospel and its relationship to culture, see Boot, *Gospel Culture*.

[2] Klaas Schilder, *Gold, Frankincense and Myrrh: Daily Meditations on the Bible for Reformation of Family, Church and State*, Vol. 1 (Neerlandia, AB: Inheritance Publications, 2013), 102.

ridiculing our history and neglecting or despising great Christian leaders in our past. For the most part, we are actually far too ignorant of our history and ambivalent toward, if not contemptuous of, the past. As a consequence, today's church is in urgent need of *reviving the memory* of great Christian leaders who modelled living faith in the power of the gospel of the kingdom.

Moreover, this profound necessity is ominously evident in that the unbelieving West today has attained a level of apostasy from the Christian faith so radical that it has become *self-conscious and evangelistic*. We have, with eyes wide open, turned our backs on the faith that deeply influenced and nurtured the life and freedoms of Western nations for generations and has made us, by grace, a blessing to others. That apostasy has spread to all sectors of society and revolutionized Western cultural life with respect to everything from human identity, marriage and family, to education and law, politics, media and art. The late American scholar Evan Runner noted in the latter third of the twentieth century:

> We are called upon to live out our lives in dark and terrifying times. From the time of the French Revolution on, our days have been filled with mounting confusion on all sides, with revolutions and acts of violence that seem only to increase in tempo, in range and in intensity. For more and more people *life appears to lack any meaning*. Even in the churches great numbers of people have accommodated themselves to secular ways of living and thinking, so that the power of Satan to deceive is mighty in the world. We can understand the words of Groen Van Prinsterer, who said, "Modern society, with all its excellences, having fallen into bondage to the theory of unbelief, is increasingly being seduced into a systematic denial of the living God."[3]

In short, the hearts of people in our culture have turned from the Lord, and a compromised, *forgetful church* shares significant responsibility for this situation.

---

[3] Runner, *Walking in the Way of the Word*, 168.

COMPREHENSIVE GOSPEL WITNESS LOOKS TO THE HEART OF THE MATTER

The Scriptures declare that "out of [the heart] spring the issues of life" (Proverbs 4:23 NKJV). It is out of the abundance of the heart that people speak and live in all the arenas of human life (Luke 6:45; James 1:15). We have seen in a previous chapter that in the Bible, *the heart* is the religious centre or root of the human personality (Psalm 51:10; Ecclesiastes 3:11; Jeremiah 17:9). All of us live *coram Deo*, and are created inescapably religious by nature, because all people are responding one way or another to the Word of God. Remember, within the structure of God's creation, there is no such thing as "non-belief." Every person holds to a belief of some kind or another, whether it be Islamic, pagan, secular humanist or Christian, and everybody thinks and acts in terms of those convictions. The orientation of the heart and the faith emerging from it thus affects all human endeavours.

Materially, of course, Christians and non-Christians are not doing different things in life and culture—rather, they are doing the same things differently, because a different *directing principle* is at work. The result is that a directional antithesis emerges in all of life's activities. While fallen and unregenerate people are in the grip of an apostate religious condition, the Christian is one whose life, in principle and in its totality, has been *redirected* by the *regeneration* of the heart. As the implications of this radical redirection are faithfully worked out, everything about the life of the Christian is changed. This glorious redirection and renewal is profoundly evident in the life of William Wilberforce. He wrote:

> The grand characteristic mark of the true Christian…is his desiring to please God in all his thoughts, and words, and actions; to take the revealed word to be the rule of his belief and practice, to "let his light shine before men;" and in all things adorn the doctrine which he professes.[4]

---

4 William Wilberforce, *A Practical View of the Prevailing View of the Prevailing Religious System of Professed Christians in the Higher Middle Classes in This Country, Contrasted with Real Christianity* (Glasgow: William Collins, 1833), 378.

In this statement we get a sense of the *religious root unity* that actuated this great man's faithfulness. He had insight into the reality that his faith, by the Word of God, must direct every aspect of his life and thought. This governing motive gets to the core of what transforms the Christian who has grasped their true relation to God, his Word and their calling to service and witness in the world. This is why we must recover, treasure and emulate the legacy of faithful witnesses who have blazed a trail of obedience in the reconciliation of all things to God (2 Corinthians 5:19).

COMPREHENSIVE GOSPEL WITNESS LOOKS BACK TO LOOK FORWARD

By this reflection on our need to *recover* something lost, something modelled in history by faithful leaders, we are not driven to simply looking back with a naïve nostalgia to some imaginary past where we once had an overtly and robustly Christian cultural order that was radically transformed by the gospel. On the contrary, Wilberforce's life was marked by a bitter struggle between the truth of the Word of God, which actuated him, and the hostility to that Word which opposed him at every turn in the corridors of power and halls of high culture.[5] The fact is, even in the West, a clearly and consistently Christian culture is yet to be historically realized. We might reasonably say that historically, Western nations have been deeply influenced and shaped by Christianity and been marked by *broadly Christianized institutions*. But certainly, no one in the last four generations has lived in a consistently Christian culture. Indeed, throughout our past, the Western world has fallen *well short* of a Christian culture that *clearly rejected* attempts at a *synthesis* with humanistic religion emanating from the philosophy of ancient Greece and Rome.

This is important to note in response to those who, in the face of the marginalization and serious challenges confronting Christians today, would claim that recovering the politically and culturally-engaged witness and optimistic faith of men like Wilberforce is largely a waste of time because old Christendom is gone and we should just get over it. We are living, many allege, in a "post-Christian age,"

---

5 See William Hague, *William Wilberforce: The Life of the Great Anti-Slave Trade Campaigner* (London: Harper Perennial, 2008), 428–450.

and so Christians should abandon their efforts at gospel-centred cultural restoration in terms of Scripture and just accept that Christianity has lost the so-called "culture war." That is to say, we should recognize that we are, and will remain, just one "interest group" among many reticent and humble applicants for religious accommodation in a multicultural society. Our task now, they allege, is to simply share our hope in Jesus and point people to the *parousia*.

Leaving aside the fact that Western history and the lives of countless thousands of suffering slaves and their children would have been very different if Wilberforce had simply pointed people piously to the Second Coming, such people miss what William Wilberforce well understood in his scripturally-rooted hopes for the success of the gospel,[6] and what the theologian Loraine Boettner has pointed out, that "there has never yet been a truly Christian age, nor has so much as one nation ever been consistently Christian. The age in which we are living is *still pre-Christian*." He continues,

> That the progress of the church through these years has been slow is due to the fact that Christians in general have not taken seriously Christ's command.... The Great Commission is addressed not merely to ministers and missionaries, but to all Christians everywhere.... The command applies to parents rearing their children, to children in regard to their parents, to individuals in whatever relationship they stand to their neighbors or business or social champions, to those who teach in the schools, to employers and employees in their mutual relationships, to writers, to newsmen, to statesmen, to Christians in general regardless of occupation or station in life.[7]

---

[6] Wilberforce shared the eschatological hope of most evangelicals of his day, and the Puritans who came before him, that obedience to God led to blessings both personal and national and that a period of glorious success for the gospel lay ahead in history—today typically called post-millennialism. When Britain abolished the slave trade in 1807 he declared "God will bless this country" and the greatest period of blessing and success called the Victorian Age followed. For a consideration of Wilberforce's eschatological hope and theological motivations, see Murray Andrew Pura, *Vital Christianity: The Life and Spirituality of William Wilberforce* (Tain, Rosshire: Christian Focus, 2003), 25–26, 72, 89–91.

[7] Loraine Boettner, *The Millennium* (Phillipsburg, NJ: Presbyterian & Reformed, 1957).

If Wilberforce and Boettner are right, and I believe they are, that we are still in a *pre-Christian* age, then world history is still moving toward the morning of gospel renewal, not falling off into the night of despair and ruin where we all may as well say, "Forget Christendom, the magisterial Reformation and the great Christian reformers of the past with their holy discontent with the status quo—those days of hope are over." Rather we must *recover* the faith of men like Wilberforce that declares Jesus Christ reigns as Lord and King. He governs history and is ruling the nations at God's right hand. Today he calls his people to be more than conquerors through him, teaching and making disciples of the nations by faith and obedience (Matthew 28:16–20).

There is no doubt, as Wilberforce himself experienced, that a pre-Christian age means very difficult times for believers, where the battle is fierce, discouragement abounds and people's hearts may fail them for fear. But history awaits faithful men and women, enlivened by the Word-revelation of God and filled with his Spirit, who will go to battle for God's glory as Christ makes darkness flee away (1 Corinthians 15:25–28). To bear witness in our times with valour, we must recover a living and *applied faith* for all of life, and for this we need to consider the lives of brave saints whose faith we can emulate. We must glance back to advance into our future.

COMPREHENSIVE GOSPEL WITNESS HAS COURAGE FOR THE CONFLICT

William Wilberforce is clearly one such evangelical example. He was a man who proved that faithfulness in times of apostasy looks like courage! Many great Christians have similarly understood the critical need for the fortitude to live *an integral life of faith in terms of the totality of God's Word.* Such lives have regularly manifested incredible social, cultural and political fruit—the remnants of which we are still feeding on today. Wilberforce himself, though best remembered for his lifelong battle with (and final victory over) a slave trade which trafficked in stolen Africans—a serious crime which carries the death penalty in Scripture (cf. Exodus 21:16; Deuteronomy 24:7; 1 Timothy 1:10)—was also one of the key founders of British evangelicalism, with a deep understanding of both the covenant Word of God and the centrality and applicability of that Word to *all of life.* Moreover, he grasped these vital truths in a time of religious regression and decline, and amid rising danger for believers in revolution-ary Europe. Thus, his immediate context demanded courage if his witness was to be faithful.

In his important book, *A Practical View of Christianity*, he prophet-ically foresaw the evils that would spill out of the French Revolution:

> A brood of moral vipers, as it were, is now hatching, which, when they shall have attained their mischievous maturity, will go forth to poison the world. But fruitless will be all attempts to sustain, much more to revive, the fainting cause of morals, unless you can in some degree restore the prevalence of evangel-ical Christianity.[8]

Though Wilberforce viewed the French Revolution and Napoleonic Wars as a permitted judgment of God upon the sins of Britain and other European nations, he clearly saw that revolutionary thought and its attendant socio-cultural decay were rooted, not in a desire for a return to Christ's lordship in cultural life, but in *religious apos-tasy*—a spirit which could not be overcome by merely military, political or social means. Yet this insight did not lead him to sit on his hands in political and cultural life, quite the contrary. He rightly perceived that what was needed *alongside* undaunted Christian cultural action was a concurrent renewal of radical faith in Christ Jesus as Lord, applied in one's life. Merely claiming to be "religious," with a personal faith and morality was not enough for Christians who wanted to bear witness to the kingdom of God with faith and courage in challenging days. Wilberforce wrote:

> We should cease to be deceived by superficial appearances, and to confound the gospel of Christ with the systems of philoso-phers; we should become impressed with that weighty truth, so much forgotten in the present day, that Christianity calls on us, as we value our immortal souls, not merely in *general*, to be *religious* and *moral*, but *specially* to believe the doctrines, imbibe the principles, and practise the precepts of Christ.... [Christi-anity] is spoken of as light from darkness, as release from prison,

---

[8] Wilberforce, *A Practical View of Christianity*, 398.

as deliverance from captivity, as life from death.... And, short as is the form of prayer taught us by our blessed Saviour, the more general extension of the kingdom of Christ constitutes one of its leading petitions.[9]

Without neglecting the truth that the covenant of grace is the cardinal point on which Christianity turns, Wilberforce understood the Christian gospel to be something eminently practical. Biographer Garth Lean notes that for Wilberforce, "it was not enough to profess Christianity, to go to church on Sundays and to live a decent life.... Christianity must be allowed to pervade and penetrate every corner of a Christian's existence."[10] We have noted that a steep trajectory away from a vital and *applied scriptural faith* was very apparent in Wilberforce's age, hence his relentless emphasis upon it. It is astonishing to read Bishop J. C. Ryle, writing descriptively of Wilberforce's debauched era:

> England seems barren of all that is really good. How such a state of things can have arisen in a land of free bibles and professing Protestantism is almost past comprehension. Christianity seems to lie as one dead. Morality, however much exalted in pulpits, is thoroughly trampled under foot in the streets. There is darkness in the court, the Parliament, and the bar...a gross, thick, religious and moral darkness...that might be felt. It may suffice to say that adultery, sexual immorality, gambling, swearing, Sabbath-breaking and drunkenness are hardly regarded vices at all. They are the fashionable practices of people in the highest ranks of society, and no one is thought the worse of for indulging in them. And what were the churches doing? Well, they exist but they could hardly be said to be alive. They do nothing; they are sound asleep.... When such is the state of things in churches and chapels, it can surprise no one to learn that the land is deluged with infidelity and scepticism.[11]

---

9 Wilberforce, *A Practical View of Christianity*, 100–101.

10 Garth Lean, *God's Politician: William Wilberforce's Struggle* (Trowbridge: Darton, Longman and Todd, 2007), 126.

11 J. C. Ryle, *Christian Leaders of the 18th Century* (Carlisle, PA: Banner of Truth Trust, 1978).

In such an environment Wilberforce was taken hold of by God's grace, gripped by his Word and Spirit, and raised up to do battle for the culture of Christ—for the liberties and beauty of the gospel—that is, to bear witness to the *kingdom of God*. This meant integrated faithful service that encompassed everything from personal evangelism and preaching to political and cultural reform, which he called the "reformation of manners."

His courageous passion for the kingdom of Christ was a theological inheritance that he had received from his evangelical forebears—the Puritans—whom he keenly read throughout his life.[12] One Canadian Wilberforce biographer, seeing the connection between the Puritans and Wilberforce as their vital faith and refusal to artificially divide personal piety from cultural transformation, wrote:

> Religion was not a set of rules but a life-force: a vision and compulsion which saw the beauty of a holy life and moved toward it, marveling at the possibilities and thrilling to the satisfaction of a god-centred life.... Neither the Puritans nor Wilberforce separated concern for personal holiness from concern for national holiness and national reform.[13]

Divorcing personal piety from the rest of one's life in the world, personal reform and renewal from the necessity of cultural restoration and national reform, especially in a time of apostasy, is not only to artificially divide one's life by a false and unscriptural dichotomy, it is to trade cowardice for courage if done against our better knowledge. Wilberforce refused the path of least resistance, and rejected the false dualism of a compromised Christianity. By grace God had prepared Wilberforce to stand fast in the eye of the storm with an undivided heart and life. We now turn to glimpse what that preparation looked like.

COMPREHENSIVE GOSPEL WITNESS CONTRIBUTES TO THE MAKING OF THE MAN

Wilberforce was born August 24, 1759 into a wealthy merchant family in the north of England, and like the illustrious Puritan political

12 Pura, *Vital Christianity*, 69.
13 Pura, *Vital Christianity*, 96.

reformer and head of state Oliver Cromwell, attended Cambridge University for a period. He was just seventeen when he arrived and had little desire at that point in his life for serious study. By this time he had lost the earnest childhood faith passed to him by his aunt Hannah and uncle William—with whom he had lived for a while after the death of his father around young William's ninth birthday. These relatives, for whom he developed a great affection, were earnest evangelicals personally acquainted with the great Methodist preacher George Whitefield, under whose ministry they had been converted. However, as a result of his demise into religious skepticism, William spent much of his youth in a dissolute lifestyle and fell in with a crowd at Cambridge engaged in gambling, partying and what he called "shapeless idleness." And while he would come to regret this juvenile time-wasting, in the providence of God he did build some important and close friendships at Cambridge, in particular with Isaac Milner, who would play a key role in his conversion, and William Pitt, the future prime minister.

Acquitting himself reasonably well in his college exams and determined to enter political life, in 1780 the witty, eloquent and naturally gifted Wilberforce successfully stood for election in his hometown of Hull—aged twenty-one and still technically a student. He soon became one of the rising stars in Parliament, where his natural speaking ability was readily noticed. William Pitt the Younger said that Wilberforce possessed "the greatest natural eloquence of all the men I ever knew." In 1784 Wilberforce stood again for election, this time leaving the safe seat of Hull for an influential seat in Yorkshire—the largest county in England. Because of his political connections, inherited wealth, personal warmth and brilliant social ability with the land-owning class, he won the seat. And so, by the time a very wealthy and politically independent Wilberforce was twenty-five, he was a member of Parliament for one of the most prestigious seats in the country and his good friend, William Pitt, was about to become prime minister. It is easy to see in hindsight how God was moving his unsuspecting servant into position.

Religiously, Wilberforce had by now adopted a kind of fashionable rationalistic Unitarianism which completely rejected orthodox Christian truth—including the divinity of Christ and the authority of Scripture. Here was a faith in a benign benevolence, acceptable to cultural elites, which made no real demands. However, in the providence of God his old friend from Cambridge, Isaac Milner, a Christian scholar and something of an apologist, ended up accompanying Wilberforce on a tour of Europe. Milner was a competent and thoughtful man who was able to articulate the heart of Christianity in a winsome manner on their journey. And so, by the summer of 1785, Wilberforce's many intellectual doubts and objections to the Christian faith had been removed, though he had not yet surrendered his heart and life to Christ. Over the next year he gradually came to place his faith completely in Christ. Yet at the time, due to the significant influence of dualistic Greek philosophy on Christianity in the West, one of his major considerations and concerns was whether he could become a faithful evangelical Christian and yet *remain in politics*. Wasn't politics a profane and "secular" vocation? Could he really surrender to Christ and remain a politician?

Nagged by these concerns, and with some trepidation over his political future if discovered going to such an appointment, Wilberforce arranged to meet with the only evangelical clergyman his wider family had some acquaintance with in London—John Newton, the former slave-trader and author of the hymn "Amazing Grace." Newton was a man Wilberforce remembered from his childhood days in Wimbledon living with his uncle and aunt. By God's grace, in a conversation of incredible historical importance, Newton not only told Wilberforce he had never ceased to pray for him, he also persuaded Wilberforce that he *could* be a faithful Christian *and* remain in politics. He later offered him the examples of Joseph and Daniel and told him, "It is hoped and believed that the Lord has raised you up for the good of his church and for the good of the nation."[14]

By Easter 1786, what Wilberforce called his "grand change" was complete. He wrote, "the promises and offers of the gospel produced in me something of a settled peace of conscience. I devoted myself for whatever might be the term of my future life, to the service of my God and Saviour."[15] Both William Pitt and John Newton played a

---

[14] John Newton, cited in Robert Isaac Wilberforce and Samuel Wilberforce, *The Life of William Wilberforce*, abridged ed. (London: 1843), 48.

[15] William Wilberforce, cited in Kevin Belmonte, *William Wilberforce: The Friend of Humanity* (Malta: Day One Publications, 2006), 43.

significant role in Wilberforce coming to see that that service needed to be in *political life*. Once settled on his course, he quickly set about mending some broken relationships he had in Parliament and soon after discovered the two great objects to which God had called him—the abolition of the slave trade and the moral reformation of the nation.

THE POWER OF HIS LIFE AND MESSAGE

When considering Wilberforce's remarkable career, it should be remembered that in the 1790s Great Britain was in a conflict for its very life and survival. It wasn't until she defeated Napoleon at the Battle of Waterloo in 1815, that the catastrophe and prolonged hardship of war with France was ended. Those years had been no easy time for William to pursue the cause of abolition or domestic moral and cultural renewal. And yet it was during this turbulent period of conflict that Wilberforce and his friends achieved their most important reforms. Furthermore, in 1797 his book, *A Practical View of Christianity*, was published to great acclaim, becoming the veritable *manifesto* of the evangelical movement in Britain and propelling their efforts across party lines and class distinction. It remained a bestseller for fifty years and marked a significant beginning of the influence of evangelicalism on the upper classes. Parliamentary luminaries of the stature of Edmund Burke were deeply impacted by it. He spent much of the last two days of his life reading it and spoke of the overwhelming comfort it brought him. The power of Wilberforce's book was in its obvious sincerity: an essay by a man whose life modelled a living faith at a time of national crisis.

The extraordinary and very challenging life of Wilberforce is a truly amazing and inspiring story that every Christian should read. The abolition of the slave trade for which he is most remembered would take the rest of his life, through much hardship, persecution, sickness and sorrow. John Wesley, the redoubtable evangelical Methodist preacher and reformer, understood the faith and perseverance that Wilberforce would require in order to accomplish his goals, and in one of the final actions of his life, aged eighty-eight, he wrote his last-ever letter to the young Wilberforce on February 24, 1791:

Unless the divine Power has raised you up to be Athanasius *contra mundum* I see not how you can go through your glorious enterprise.... Unless God has raised you up for this very thing, you will be worn out by the opposition of man and devils. But if God is for you, who can be against you. Are all of them together stronger than God? O be not weary of well doing! Go on, in the name of God and in the power of his might, till even American slavery (the vilest that ever saw the sun) shall vanish away before it.[16]

By God's grace and against all the odds, Wilberforce finally succeeded in getting his abolition bill passed into law. In fact, February 23, 1807, became one of the most important nights in British political history. As speeches were made that momentous evening, incredible tributes were heaped upon Wilberforce—the high point being when Sir Samuel Romilly rose to contrast the achievement of Napoleon with that of Wilberforce, a man who could put his head on the pillow that night knowing the infamy of the slave trade was done away. After years of political hostility, conflict and opposition, the House stood and applauded exuberantly as Wilberforce wept, his head in his hands.

Yet the abolition of the slave trade was just one of Wilberforce's many gospel-centred social and political accomplishments. He was hugely influential in a wide variety of cultural developments in Britain. His measures included desperately-needed reform. At the political level, he pursued the revision of an inhumane penal code to reduce the number of death penalties and hangings, while with royal approval he established the Society for the Suppression of Vice. Royal proclamations for the encouragement of piety and suppression of vice were issued. At the same time he challenged a corrupt church establishment by assaulting the idle "buck parsons," living off the church and wearying the people. The impact of Wilberforce and his friends was so great that churches began filling up again; family prayers were increasingly being held in the homes of all classes; even

---

[16] John Wesley, *Letters of John Wesley,* a selection of important and new letters, with introductions and biographical notes by George Eayrs (New York: Hodder and Stoughton, 1915), 489–490.

WILLIAM WILBERFORCE, AGED 29
(1759–1833)[†]

[†]Artist: John Rising (1753–1817); public domain.

Princess Victoria was given an evangelical tutor by the Duke of Kent. It is estimated that shortly thereafter, influenced by Wilberforce's reforms, around 8 per cent of Anglican clergy were evangelical. Indeed, the social order and missional vitality of the Victorian age is impossible to imagine without William Wilberforce and his evangelical life of faith.[17]

It must be stressed that Wilberforce did not accomplish these almost miraculous feats alone. The lifelong friends that *gathered around him*, called the Clapham Sect, laboured together for the kingdom of Christ. One historian wrote that:

> They possessed between them an astonishing range of capacities: encyclopaedic knowledge, a capacity for research, sparkling wit and literary style, business sagacity, foreign policy expertise, legal ability, oratory and parliamentary skill. No prime minister had such a cabinet as Wilberforce could summon to his assistance.[18]

At one point, Wilberforce was said to be involved in over sixty different ministries; he was instrumental in founding the British and Foreign Bible Society for the distribution of Scripture, the Church Missionary Society, the Sunday School Society and schools for the poor. He even set up the RSPCA (The Royal Society for the Prevention of Cruelty to Animals). Through his evangelical friend Hannah Moore, Wilberforce and the Clapham Sect established schools in the West Country and educated thousands of children. They began lending libraries, soup kitchens and schools for the deaf and blind. They sponsored smallpox vaccinations and campaigned for shorter working hours and better conditions in factories. They purchased the release of those in prison for debt and, in advancing arts and culture, they helped found the National Gallery. Wilberforce visited prisons with the distinguished Elizabeth Fry and funded hospitals and endless causes for poverty relief, as well as campaigning for the humane treatment of Native Americans and

---

[17] Lean, *God's Politician*, 83.
[18] Lean, *God's Politician*, 104.

the people of India. He gave away vast swathes of his personal fortune till at the end of his life very little remained. As historian John Pollock put it so well, "William Wilberforce is proof that a man can change his times, though he cannot do it alone."[19]

Yet Wilberforce knew well that the kingdom of God and our witness to it is not simply a matter of passionate and fervent activity. As Wesley warned Wilberforce, pursuing godly cultural reformation by our own resources and strength, as though cultural action alone were sufficient, would be a great mistake ending in exhaustion and disappointment. Wilberforce understood that there would be no preservation of truth and justice, nor the growth of Christian cultural order, without a transformation of hearts and minds—beginning with the individual. As Charles Colson has correctly pointed out:

> Wilberforce ultimately prevailed because he understood the futility of attempting to end a systemic evil without also changing citizens' values and dispositions. He knew he not only had to work for justice; he also had to convince people of the need for the moral consensus that flowed from a biblical worldview.[20]

There can be no lasting change without the transformation and renewal of people's minds providing a common foundation for social order. As Lord Hague, a politician, historian and Wilberforce biographer has noted, "Wilberforce was a legislator for almost the whole of his adult life, but central to his beliefs was the view that laws must be underpinned by a common understanding of ethics and conduct."[21] William understood that this common understanding must be grounded in the gospel of Christ.

---

[19] John Pollock, *William Wilberforce: A Man who Changed his Times* (MacLean, VA: Trinity Forum, 2006), 88.

[20] Charles Colson and Anne Morse, "The Wilberforce Strategy," *Christianity Today* 51, no. 2 (2007): 132.

[21] Hague, *William Wilberforce*, 514.

COMPREHENSIVE GOSPEL WITNESS LEAVES
A LEGACY OF FAITH

Wilberforce lived in difficult and demanding times, but he perse-
vered in faith and obedience. He died in 1833, just days after slavery
was finally abolished in every corner of the British Empire. At his
funeral was a man who admired him greatly and continued his legacy
of faith and action, Anthony Ashley Cooper, 7th Earl of Shaftesbury,
who would become the champion of Britain's industrial poor, saving
child labourers from Britain's mines and factories. As Murray Andrew
Pura writes of Wilberforce, "He who became a moral father to his
country and the conscience of England also became a father and a
guiding conscience to a spiritual movement that has largely been
forgotten."[22]

Today we live again in frightening and challenging times requiring
new fathers in the faith ready to follow the example of Wilberforce
and be a prophetic voice to the nation. Though historical compari-
sons are quite difficult and variable, it is safe to say that the depth of
need and religious apostasy in our present culture easily rivals that
of Wilberforce's era, since our age is marked by a self-conscious and
deliberate rejection of God's creational order, scriptural faith and our
Christian heritage. We face opposition and challenges on every side,
with the historic freedom to witness openly and publicly to the truth
of the gospel under increasing legal threat. Wickedness so often
seems to prevail in our society. However, we have no reason to lose
hope. The early disciples confronted the seemingly impenetrable
religious colossus of the Greco-Roman world, and understood that
kingdom faithfulness was their obligation, despite the seeming
impossibility of the task.

The joy and hope that is ours as believers, whatever the opposition,
resides in the fact that Christ is with us (Matthew 28:20), and "if
God is for us, who can be against us?" (Romans 8:31) The calling of
believers to gospel witness is accomplished by the work of Christ in
and through his people—we are simply called to walk in obedience
and leave the results to God (Philippians 2:13). Regeneration, restoration and even cultural renewal are not ultimately our work. Life,
truth and justice can only prevail when a *new direction in the religious*

---

[22] Pura, *Vital Christianity*, 141.

root of man's being—the heart—takes shape and his *life and thinking are renewed* in terms of the living Word of God. At the same time the Christian is not called to passivity. It is *because* God's law-Word is sovereign and Jesus Christ is Lord, that we as his image bearers and co-heirs, his new humanity, are commissioned to bear witness to the truth in word and deed, serving the culture of Christ. As Albert Wolters states:

> God's rule of law is immediate in the nonhuman realm but mediate in culture and society. In the human realm men and women become coworkers with God; as creatures made in God's image they too have a kind of lordship over the earth, are God's viceroys in creation.[23]

By his self-conscious dependence on the Holy Spirit, Wilberforce's life reveals that faithful gospel witness and kingdom transformation requires glad service to the Word of God in every area of life, from family life and education, evangelism and preaching, to political, cultural and charitable engagement. This great man's life shows us that a radical and *integral faith* in Christ's total lordship requires an *integral witness* that leaves no area untouched by the power of the Word of God. This is Wilberforce's legacy and the secret of his great influence.

The church in our day urgently needs to be resourced by the example and wisdom of men like Wilberforce, and this requires knowing their context, their motivation and their biblical faith. We need to imitate this faith and by so doing mark a new starting point, finding new vigour, fresh clarity and a recovered scriptural basis for thought and action rooted in the lordship of Christ.

In this glorious witness-bearing to the kingdom of God our hope is not in human effort, but in the omnipotent working of the Holy Spirit and the *power of the gospel*. An aging Wilberforce reflected this confidence at the end of his life when he wrote:

> I must confess...that my own solid hopes for the wellbeing of my country depend not so much on her navies and armies, nor

---

[23] Wolters, *Creation Regained*, 16

on the wisdom of her rulers, nor on the spirit of her people, but on the persuasion that she still contains many who love and obey the Gospel of Christ. I believe that their prayers may yet prevail.[24]

In such a hope we *shall prevail* because Jesus Christ is Lord, and the God of peace shall soon crush Satan under our feet.

[24] Wilberforce, *A Practical View of Christianity*, ix.

Also available from Ezra Press…

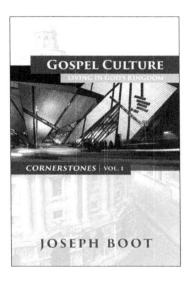

CORNERSTONES | VOL. I
GOSPEL CULTURE: LIVING IN GOD'S KINGDOM
JOSEPH BOOT

Culture is something we build, something we do with creation; it is the outward expression of a people's *worship*, in terms of which they cultivate their society, including its law, education, arts and customs and much more besides. Whether we realize it or not, we all participate daily in culture-building of one form or another. The *gospel of the kingdom* is the good news that Jesus Christ is King of kings and Lord of lords, and that he is at work to redeem this fallen world, remaking it in accordance with his good purposes. To speak of gospel culture, then, is to speak of a total meaning for the cosmos, a design plan. The gospel has something to say about the way we go about all our cultural activities. God's Word is a total structuration of life and thought. If we would see Jesus Christ honoured and worshipped, if we would see our Lord's will done on earth as it is in heaven, then we must faithfully consider the scriptural view of the gospel and its implications for culture. **ISBN 978-0-9947279-1-6**

WWW.EZRAINSTITUTE.CA

Made in the USA
Las Vegas, NV
29 November 2022

60645097R00089